Monday Morning Meditations

Monday Morning Meditations

Reflections of a Parish Priest

Steven C. Kostoff

KALOROS PRESS
Wadmalaw Island, South Carolina
2018

Copyright © 2018 Steven C. Kostoff

ISBN 978-1-937019-94-5

To my wife and co-minister,

Presvytera Deborah

Contents

Introduction	1
September	
The Church New Year: Curing the Summertime Blues	5
The Nativity of the Theotokos and Its Synaxis: Remembering Sts Joachim and Anna	8
"Wood Is Healed by Wood"	11
Before Thy Cross, We Bow Down in Worship!	15
Glory to God for Autumn	18
October	
"Let us Attend!"	22
Tribulation in this Life	26
"God or Nothing"	30
Moving beyond Mere Belief	33
November	
Eucharistic Beings in a Eucharistic Society	36
Forty Shopping (and Fasting) Days until Christmas	39
Indulging Not in Food, But in Giving Thanks to the Lord	42
Preparing for the Incarnation	46
December	
The Image of Giving in St Nicholas	49
In the Fullness of Time	52
Christmas and Martyrdom	56
The Incarnation: A Word about the Word	59
The Time of Our Lives	62
January	
Redeeming the Time	65
Baptism: "When All Is Said and Done"	69
Rebuking the Tempter and Following Jesus	73
A "Pouring Out of Long Accumulating, Long Pent-up Pain"	77
Ascending with Zacchaeus	81
February	
If St John Chrysostom Had Watched the Super Bowl	84
An Infant's Burial	89
The Heresy of the Rapture	93
Now Is the Acceptable Time: Lent as Beginning	96

March

On the Liturgy of St Basil the Great	100
To Refresh Our Souls and Encourage Us	104
The Announcement of the Incarnation	108
The Real Stairway to Heaven	111

April

Acedia, Us, and Our Lenten Effort	115
Holy Week: A Mystic Torrent	119
The Resurrection of Christ and the Rise of Christianity	122
Paschal Reminiscences	132

May

"Lent after Lent" and "Life after Pascha"	136
Death's Dominion Has Been Shattered!	139
"Do You Want to Be Healed?"	143
Mid-Pentecost: "Glistening with Splendor"	146
From Where Do We Draw Our Water?	149

June

Too Busy NOT to Pray	153
Forty-Nine Plus One: Pentecost and the Life beyond Time	155
The Day of the Holy Spirit	158
Finding our "Self" in the Other: Reflections on National Selfie Day	163

July

July: A Month-Long Spiritual Desert	168
Bored by Sin	171
Blessed Dissatisfaction	176
A Feast of Divine Beauty	180

August

The Dormition Fast: Commitment Versus Convenience	183
The Awesome God and the Transfigured Life	186
Rejoicing in the "Deathless Death"	189
Rejoicing in All that Is Good	193

Appendix: Reading the Meditations through the Liturgical Year	196

Introduction

It was now many years ago – in the late 1990s, I would say – when I sat down at the computer in my church office and sent an email with the subject of "Monday Morning Meditation." This was to relatively few parishioners whose names were on my email distribution list. (From what I recall, that was still rather early, before the widespread use of email as a common mode of communication.) There was nothing premeditated about the email, it was just a thought that came to me at the moment and I hoped the use of alliteration would attract some attention. After some positive response, I continued to write these meditations with some regularity, and as my distribution list began to expand, I gradually developed something of a cyberspace ministry, for lack of a better term.

This book is, then, an anthology of some of the most perennial Monday Morning Meditations from over the years. I should clarify that I am not using the term "meditation" in any technical sense in these reflections. I strive, instead, to encourage serious readers to "be mindful" of what is contained in each selection, to think carefully about what is written, with the goal of bringing our minds and hearts back to the reality of God, whether at home or in the workplace. This can be a challenge on Monday mornings, when the words of an old song by the Mamas & the Papas, "Monday, Monday, so good to me," seem painfully unrealistic. I was thus hoping that after the weekend, when life again acquired its quotidian rhythms – when the "peace" experienced in the Liturgy with which we are exhorted to depart may have already evaporated – that a few words about a scriptural passage, or some insights from our theological, spiritual, or liturgical tradition as expressed by the saints, may have the effect of awakening us to the mindfulness of God. The further hope is that any such meditation would serve to bridge the gap, or even disconnect, between "liturgy and life," to use an expression from Fr Alexander Schmemann.

That perceived gap may have something to do with how Monday is seen in our approach to the unending weekly cycle of days that comprises one of our most basic experiences of time. Sunday is the first day of the week, technically speaking, but on the level of popular perception, the week begins with *Monday*. From that perspective, the weekend comes at the end of the work week, which naturally begins again on the following Monday. And this perception of the weekly cycle has managed to endure, although today people increasingly work on the weekends. Obviously, the weakening consciousness of Sunday as the Lord's Day and thus the first – and eighth! – day of the week following the "Sabbath" in our secularized society has a great deal to do with this.

As Christians are fully integrated into the world today, such a perception can shape our own approach toward the weekly cycle and create that disconnect alluded to above as we are tempted to compartmentalize our "religious" and "secular" lives. In attempting to pastorally address that possible disconnect, I was hoping that a short, modest Monday morning meditation would be beneficial. As the work week begins and as our computer screens light up at work or home, perhaps a few words concerning God will serve to broaden our perspective while reminding us of our encounter with Christ on the previous day.

On the whole, the meditations gathered here follow the liturgical calendar and the annual cycles of fasting and feasting in the Church, and the reader is encouraged to take advantage of this by reading one meditation each Monday of the year. Although some meditations address a topic of general interest and are therefore not connected to a specific time on the church calendar, even in those cases, a conscious attempt was made to find an appropriate season for each meditation. Thus, the first meditation centers on the ecclesiastical New Year on September 1, and the subsequent selections continue through the fixed and moveable cycles of the calendar. To navigate the paschal cycle, or for a better idea of when to read each meditation during the liturgical year, please refer to the appendix.

In that regard, I would like to offer my heartfelt thanks to my former parishioner, Dr Nicole Roccas, for her excellent editorial work in preparing the initial draft, for providing the initial stimulus to begin this endeavor and for compiling the appendix. I would like to extend my deepest appreciation to Michael Breck, managing director of Kaloros Press, for his warm and professional support in bringing this work to fruition. And also to Fr John Breck for his consistent encouragement throughout the years to "keep on writing."

Continuing to write these pastoral reflections over the years has been a great source of enjoyment for me, and if anyone finds something worthwhile in these modest meditations, that would prove to be a further source of gladness.

The First Monday of September
Originally Written: August 2015

The Church New Year: Curing the Summertime Blues

The Spirit of the Lord GOD is upon me,
...to proclaim the year of the LORD's favor.
(Is 61.1–2; cf. Lk 4.18–19)

The first day of September marks the beginning of the Church year. This is an overlooked commemoration, but with more attention, it can become an important day in our ecclesial lives – it is a new beginning, and beginnings present us with the possibility of starting fresh, if not starting over. It can be an opportunity for a genuine "re-orientation," which literally means to be directed back toward the East, the "orient." The East is symbolically connected to the rising light of Christ, the Sun of Righteousness (cf. Mal 4.2), and was the direction early Christians faced in prayer. As such, the act of turning eastward is associated with repentance. If the summer was a time of being scattered here and there, the ecclesiastical New Year is a gathering together of the soul and body to redirect our lives toward Christ once again. Curiously, it is only now that some begin to attend church regularly again – the "vacation" from God and church is over and now is the time to embrace a more serious liturgical rhythm. Thus, while the Eddie Cochran song laments "there ain't no cure for the summertime blues," we can proclaim that there is – in the Church.

As the beginning of the Church year, September 1 prepares us for the annual liturgical cycle of feast days. Perhaps more specifically, it reinstates the rhythm of fasting and feasting that immerses us into the counter-cultural life of the Church and challenges the patterns, attitudes, and emptiness of the secular culture that surrounds us. Instead of a hectic life based on competition and consumerism, we encounter the grace-filled life of the Church based on cooperation and communion. The world (which in this context connotes a life directed toward the self and consumed with the passions) offers us the kingdom of mammon, while the Church offers us the kingdom of God. Much of our lives is spent in tension between the two kingdoms – in our fallen-ness, we often lack the courage to choose the better path. Yet, our inability to make a firm choice between the two is rather amazing when one contemplates the two choices – as another song says, you "can't get no satisfaction" from mammon (Rolling Stones). Mammon is eventually consumed by "moth and rust" (Mt 6.19). Although the gifts of the kingdom are imperishable, the pull of the world nonetheless stretches us in so many conflicting directions it often feels like we are trapped in a labyrinth. We lose our way at times. We struggle with choices. It is a veritable "bungle in the jungle," as yet another song says. However, the Church's vision of Christ and His kingdom gives us the opportunity to live out the familiar yet meaningful maxim: be in the world but not of the world (see Jn 15.19, 17.14–16).

Immersing ourselves in the life of the Church, to the extent that it is possible for each of us, is a way to clarify our vision and make an honest attempt to be kingdom-oriented Christians. As Fr Lev Gillet has written:

> In the liturgical year we are called to relive the whole life of Christ: from Christmas to Easter, from Easter to Pentecost, we are exhorted to unite ourselves to Christ in His birth and in His growth, to Christ suffering, to Christ dying, to Christ in triumph and to Christ inspiring His Church. The liturgical year forms Christ in us, from His birth to full stature of the perfect man.*

---

* A Monk of the Eastern Church, *The Year of Grace of the Lord: A Scriptural and*

With a bit of planning and prioritizing, we can make that immersion a greater reality in our lives. Instead of hanging up our Church calendars as pious adornments or reminders of an archaic way of life, we can utilize them as a means of directing us toward life in Christ. From feast days and daily commemorations to scriptural readings, our liturgical calendars are like maps, revealing the location of true treasure worth digging for. Without exhausting ourselves in the process, we do not have to lose the "battle of the calendars," if I may use that expression. Life consists of daily choices, some of which can direct us toward the Church. I am not advocating an artificial division between "religious" and "secular" life – the point is not to choose one and ignore the other. That would only be a form of compartmentalization foreign to the Gospel, which resoundingly affirms our whole life has been redeemed. For the believing Christian, there is only one life – that which is "in Christ" – and that is the life we offer in obedience to the Lord and master of our lives, Jesus Christ. Christianity is not one religion among others, but rather an all-encompassing way of life that embraces the Liturgy, our homes, and the workplace: essentially it touches everything that sets us apart as human beings. Nonetheless, making the Gospel the cornerstone of our lives establishes a hierarchy of values in which all reality has its place. This new vision of life becomes clearer when we begin to "reorient" our lives to face Christ and His Church.

> Behold, now is the acceptable time; behold now is the day of salvation. (2 Cor 6.2)

Liturgical Commentary on the Calendar of the Orthodox Church (Crestwood, NY: St Vladimir's Seminary Press, 1980), 2.

The Second Monday of September
Originally Written: September 2013

The Nativity of the Theotokos and Its Synaxis: Remembering Sts Joachim and Anna

Following the ecclesiastical New Year, the first major feast is the Nativity of the Theotokos (September 8). It allows us a good start to the liturgical year unfolding before us. In this straightforward and joyous feast devoted to the birth of the Virgin Mary, we receive a taste of the joyous life within the Church that life's challenges and tragedies so often deaden:

> In and through this newborn girl, Christ – our gift from God, our meeting and encounter with Him – comes to embrace the world. Thus, in celebrating Mary's birth we find ourselves already on the road to Bethlehem, moving toward the joyful mystery of Mary as the Mother of God.[*]

In an age of cynicism, sin tends to obscure the awareness of life's inherent goodness. When we can no longer see the blessings around us, we lose something vital to our humanity. The only cure for this is repentance, embracing a changed mind to transform our humanity. To encounter the purity of the Theotokos is to see life with this kind of restored vision. She reminds us that faithfulness and purity of heart are embodied realities lived by actual human beings. This renewed awareness likewise strengthens our ability to perceive the goodness around us. Fr Schmemann emphasizes the "image of woman" the Virgin Mary reveals:

> The Virgin Mary, the All-Pure Mother demands nothing and receives everything. She pursues nothing, and possesses all. In the image of the Virgin Mary, we find what

---

[*] Alexander Schmemann, *The Virgin Mary*, vol. 3 of *Celebration of Faith* (Crestwood, NY: St Vladimir's Seminary Press, 1995), 25.

has almost completely been lost in our proud, aggressive, male world: compassion, tender-heartedness, care, trust, humility. We call her our Lady and the Queen of heaven and earth, and yet she calls herself "the handmaid of the Lord." ... Beholding this woman – Virgin, Mother, Intercessor – we begin to sense, to know not with our mind but with our heart, what it means to seek the Kingdom, to find it, and to live by it.[*]

Some will undoubtedly see nothing but a stereotype of the feminine in this description, but I believe the tender humility of the Theotokos lends a vital balance to our faith.

The day after the Nativity (September 9) is the "synaxis" of Joachim and Anna, the father and mother of the Virgin Mary, according to Church tradition. This reflects a consistent pattern within our liturgical commemorations – on the day following certain feasts, we remember those persons who were integral to that feast day's events. After Theophany, for example, we commemorate St John the Baptist; after the Nativity of Christ, we remember the Theotokos. Similarly, because of the essential role played by Joachim and Anna in the Virgin Mary's birth, we can meditate on their important place in this festal commemoration.

The source of their respective roles is the *Protoevangelion of James*, a mid-second-century document that, as Kallistos Ware explains, is not placed "on the same level as Holy Scripture" in the Orthodox Church. "It is possible, then, to accept the spiritual truth which underlies this narrative, without necessarily attributing a literal and historical exactness to every detail."[**]

One of the spiritual truths to which Kallistos alludes is the *Protoevangelion*'s account that Joachim and Anna continued to pray with

---

[*] Ibid., 21-22.
[**] Mother Mary and Archimandrite Kallistos Ware, *The Festal Menaion* (London: Faber & Faber, 1969), 47.

faith and trust in God's providence, even though they were greatly discouraged over Anna's barrenness.* A lack of children in ancient Israel was often interpreted as a sign of God's displeasure, an indication of hidden sins that deserved rebuke. Though disheartened, Joachim and Anna continued to place their trust in God, refusing to turn away from God though their patience was thoroughly tested. Persevering prayer in the face of discouragement is a spiritual feat that reveals genuine faith. Their trust in God culminated in the conception and birth of the Virgin Mary. Perhaps this is why we commemorate Joachim and Anna as the "ancestors of God" at the conclusion of every major liturgical service, including the Divine Liturgy – we seek their prayers as icons of an everyday faith expressed by fidelity, faith, and trust in God's providential care.

Joachim and Anna are also examples of a genuine conjugal love. Their union is an image of a chaste sexual love devoid of lust and self-seeking pleasure. The strong ascetical emphases of many celibate saints sometimes eclipse, albeit unintentionally, the blessings of conjugal love as envisaged in the sacrament of marriage. In fact, through its canonical legislation going back to the early centuries of Christianity, the Church has struggled against a distorted asceticism that denigrates sexual love even within the bounds of marriage. The Church is not "anti-sex," so to speak, but challenges us to discern the qualitative distinction between love and lust. The icon of the embrace of Joachim and Anna outside the gates of their home as they both rush to embrace each other following the exciting news that they would indeed be given a child, is the image of this purified conjugal love. Ultimately, their love resulted in the birth of Mary, who was conceived as all other children are. The Feast of the Nativity of the Theotokos has four days of afterfeast, its leavetaking occurs on September 12. This allows us to prepare for the Feast of the Elevation of the Cross shortly thereafter, on September 14.

* See Frederica Mathewes-Green, *The Lost Gospel of Mary: The Mother of Jesus in Three Ancient Texts* (Brewster, MA: Paraclete Press, 2013), 31-37.

The Third Monday of September
Originally Written: September 2015

"Wood Is Healed by Wood"

The Feast of the Elevation of the Cross reveals numerous biblical, historical, and theological themes on which to meditate. One such theme is a *typological* understanding of the Scriptures, a profound way of glimpsing connections between the persons, events, and places of the Old Testament – what we would call types – and their fulfillment as anti-types in the New Testament. Thus, Adam is a type of which Christ – the new Adam – is the anti-type: "Adam, who was a type of the one who was to come" (Rom 5.14).

Through typology, the Old Testament can be read as anticipating the person of Christ and the saving events of the New Testament without undermining the integrity of the historical particularities surrounding ancient Israel as the people of God, entrusted by God with a messianic destiny. An example of this typological application is expressed in an intriguing and paradoxical manner in a hymn of the Feast of the Elevation of the Cross:

> For it is fitting that wood should be healed by wood, and that through the Passion of One Who knew not passion should be remitted all the suffering of him who was condemned because of wood.[*]

"Wood should be healed by wood." What a wonderful phrase, yet what is this wood to which the hymn refers? How does wood heal wood? In both instances, the wood is clearly the wood of two trees – the tree of the knowledge of good and evil (cf. Gen 2), and the

---
[*] Mother Mary and Archimandrite Kallistos Ware, *The Festal Menaion*, 134.

wood of the tree of the cross. In disobedience to the command of God, Adam and Eve ate of the tree of the knowledge of good and evil. This was the one tree, the fruit of which it was not safe for them to eat: "You may freely eat of every tree of the garden; but of the tree of the knowledge of good and evil you shall not eat, for in the day that you eat of it you shall die" (Gen 2.16–17).

The freedom and self-determination of the first man and woman were tested by this divine commandment. In a celebrated interpretation of this passage, St Gregory the Theologian († AD 395) draws out the meaning of this command and its consequences:

> God gave [Adam] a law as material on which his self-determination could work, and the law was a commandment indicating which plants he could possess and which one he was not to touch. And that was the tree of knowledge, which was neither planted from the beginning in an evil way nor forbidden through envy – let the enemies of God not wag their tongues in that direction, nor imitate the serpent – but would be good if possessed at the right time. For the tree of contemplation, according to my own contemplation, which is only safe for those who are still simpler and those greedy in their desire, just as adult food is not useful for those who are still tender and in need of milk.[*]

St Athanasius the Great († AD 373) expresses this in similar terms:

> Knowing once more how the will of man could sway to either side, in anticipation God secured the grace given to them by a command and by the place where He put them. For He brought them into His own garden and gave them a law so that, if they kept the grace and remained good, they might still keep the life in paradise without sorrow or pain or care, besides having the promise or incorruption

---

[*] St Gregory of Nazianzus, *Festal Orations*, trans. Nonna Verna Harrison (Crestwood, NY: St Vladimir's Seminary Press, 2008), 69.

> in heaven. But if they transgressed and turned back and became evil, they might know that they were incurring that corruption in death that was theirs by nature, no longer to live in paradise but cast out of it from that time forth to die and abide in death and corruption.[*]

The initial innocence of Adam and Eve – their lack of maturity and their need for spiritual growth – is a widely referenced point in the writings of the Church fathers. As early as St Irenaeus of Lyons († c. AD 200), it was observed that: "[T]he man was a young child, not yet having a perfect deliberation and because of this he was easily deceived by the seducer."[**] Nothing created by God is evil by nature; rather, all is "very good" (Gen 1.31), but misdirected free will can pervert the good into something evil. The gift of the promise of deification is a God-sourced – not self-sourced – gift.

On the other hand, the tree of the cross is precisely the wood through which the first disobedience was undone by the one who died on it in obedience to the will of the Father. The tree of life in the garden of Eden was a type of the tree of the cross on Golgotha. Christ – the new Adam – healed us of the sin of the first Adam. (Similarly, already in the second century, St Justin Martyr described the Virgin Mary as the "new Eve" because of her obedience to the word of God.) The cross is therefore "the blessed Wood, through which the eternal justice has been brought to pass. For he who by a tree deceived our forefather Adam is by the cross himself deceived, and he who by tyranny gained possession of the creature endowed by God with royal dignity is overthrown in headlong fall."[***]

---

[*] St Athanasius, *On the Incarnation* 3.4, trans. John Behr (Crestwood, NY: St Vladimir's Seminary Press, 2011), 52.
[**] St Irenaeus of Lyons, *On the Apostolic Preaching*, trans. John Behr (Crestwood, NY: St Vladimir's Seminary Press, 1997), 47.
[***] Mother Mary and Archimandrite Kallistos Ware, *The Festal Menaion*, 134.

According to a pious tradition, the place of the skull (Golgotha) is where Adam was buried when he died. The blood that flowed from Christ on the cross – the tree of life – effectively "baptized" that skull, a symbolic gift of renewal and eternal life to the sons of Adam (and Eve). As one of the litiya hymns for the Feast of the Elevation proclaims,

> [T]he Tree of true life was planted in the place of the skull, and upon it hast Thou, the eternal King, worked salvation in the midst of the earth. Exalted today, it sanctifies the ends of the world.*

For this reason, icons of the crucifixion generally depict the cross of Christ as being planted on the skull of Adam, above which an inscription reads "the grave of Adam."

"Wood is healed by Wood." This is the good news revealed in the typological depictions of the Elevation of the Cross, together with the biblical exegesis of the Church fathers. Therefore, we honor and venerate the cross by bowing down before it in adoration. The cross is the heart of the Gospel – an instrument of shame in the ancient world, it becomes the instrument of salvation in Christ. Therefore, the Apostle Paul proclaimed the gospel to be the power of God: "For I am not ashamed of the gospel: it is the power of God for salvation to every one who has faith, to the Jew first and also to the Greek" (Rom 1.16). Just as we cannot be ashamed of the Gospel, we also cannot be ashamed of the tree of the cross through which "joy has come into the world" (*Liturgy of St John Chrysostom*).

---

* Ibid., 137.

The Fourth Monday of September
Originally Written: September 2015

Before Thy Cross, We Bow Down in Worship!

Then will appear the sign of the Son of man in heaven.
(Mt 24.30)

Contemporary scholars debate the meaning of the word "sign" in the words of Christ found in the above passage that describes His *parousia* or second coming in highly symbolic terms. This sign, whatever it may be, will be impossible to miss or misinterpret. It will overwhelm those present to observe it and stand in its shadow, so to speak. Yet, for many of the Church fathers – including St John Chrysostom – the sign in this passage refers to the cross of the Savior. Commenting on this passage, St John writes that "[t]he cross will be brighter than the sun. The sun will be darkened and hide itself. The sun will appear at times when it would not normally appear.... For his cross was drawing near, a thing that seemed to be a matter of reproach" (*The Gospel of Matthew*, Homily 79.1).*

The Church fathers were in direct continuity with the New Testament in their emphasis on the cross in the divine economy. There was no way to underemphasize or somehow evade the centrality of the cross – if Jesus was Lord, then His lordship had been fully revealed in the resurrection through His death on the cross. As we read in Acts 2.36, "Let all the house of Israel therefore know assuredly that God has made him both Lord and Christ, this Jesus whom you crucified."

* Matthew 14-28, vol. Ib of *Ancient Christian Commentary on Scripture*, ed. Manlio Simonetti (Downers Grove, IL: IVP Academic, 2002), 202, 231.

St Paul knew that the cross of the Lord was a "stumbling block to Jews and folly to Gentiles" (1 Cor 1.23). It was no different in the subsequent centuries, including the Patristic Age when the Church fathers offered their great commentaries on the Scriptures. And it is no different today: there will always remain a deep sense of incomprehension before the mystery of the cross. How can suffering and death be the path to glorification and life with God? St Paul, however, did not flinch from what God had revealed, and he drew his own hard conclusion: "For the word of the cross is folly to those who are perishing, but to us who are being saved it is the power of God" (1 Cor 1.18). Even more emphatically for the great apostle, the cross and Christ are so closely bound together that both are considered "the wisdom of God" (cf. 1 Cor 1.20–25). The cross may be "foolish," "low," and "despised" (1 Cor 1.27–28), but it is Christ Jesus, the crucified one, "whom God made our wisdom, our righteousness and sanctification and redemption" (1 Cor 1.30). St John Chrysostom, in a beautiful image, says "I call Him King because I see Him crucified."

The cross does not stand alone – it is always linked to the resurrection of Christ, which reveals the inner meaning of the cross and its fulfillment. Without the resurrection, the cross would indeed remain an instrument of suffering and death, having the "last word" in a fallen and irredeemable world. Liturgically, we express this through a powerful hymn sung on the Feast of the Elevation of the Cross: "Before Thy Cross, we bow down in worship, O Master, and Thy Holy Resurrection, we glorify!" This organic and inextricable union of the cross and resurrection is beautifully expressed in every celebration of the Liturgy, when immediately after the reception of the Eucharist we chant,

> Having beheld the Resurrection of Christ, let us worship the holy Lord Jesus, the only Sinless One. We venerate Thy cross, O Christ, and we praise and glorify Thy Holy Resurrection, for Thou art our God, and we know no other than Thee; we call on Thy name. Come all you faithful, let us

venerate Christ's holy Resurrection! For, behold, through the Cross joy has come into all the world. Let us ever bless the Lord, praising His Resurrection, for by enduring the Cross for us, He has destroyed death by death."
(*Liturgy of St John Chrysostom*)

Christians live under and by the sign of the cross. Many Christians – certainly Orthodox Christians – even make this sign over their bodies when they "cross themselves." Of course, this can become nothing but an empty gesture, the vestige of a cultural tradition that has long lost its significance. It can even be manipulated in a manner dangerously approaching superstition – as if the cross were a sort of charm or talisman that magically protects a person. However, let us assume our intentions are to treat the sign of the cross with respect and reverence. There are yet more subtle temptations to contend with. For example, we can compartmentalize our lives to the extent that we consciously or subconsciously regard so-called religion – even God – as separate from our daily lives. In doing so, we can find ourselves living under a different "sign" than that of the cross.

As we prepare to celebrate the Elevation of the Cross, let us again recommit ourselves to taking up the cross of Christ to embrace the joy and blessing that come from following Him.

The Fifth Monday of September
Originally Written: October 2004

Glory to God for Autumn

From my personal perspective, fall surpasses the rest of the four seasons in beauty. One of autumn's greatest attractions is in the flaming red, orange, yellow, and golden leaves that transform familiar trees into a series of "burning bushes," each one seemingly brighter than the last. When combined with a piercing, blue sky on a sunlit day and that autumnal crispness in the air, I find myself vividly aware of my surroundings and thankful for God's creation.

On a more philosophical note – apt to emerge, for example, on an overcast, windswept day – we may realize that the "colorful death" of fall signals the fleeting nature of everything beautiful in this world: "For the form of this world is passing away" (1 Cor 7.31). Yet, this very beauty and the yearning that accompanies it are a sign of the ineffable beauty of the coming kingdom of God.

Growing up on a typical city block in Detroit, I distinctly recall a neighborhood ritual that marked this particular season: raking and burning leaves. Every year, after the trees had lost most of their adornment, everyone on the block gathered the fallen leaves into neat mounds of color that rested alongside the curb. Once they were lit, raking turned to tending and overseeing the burning piles. This usually occurred after dinner, when it was already dark, but one could still see the shimmering waves of heat the flames gave off. They warmed us against the early evening chill as the ashes rushed upward toward the nighttime sky. Pardon my momentary indifference to the environment, but I thoroughly enjoyed those small bonfires and the pungent smell of burning leaves. As I recall, this unmistakable fragrance would linger in the air for several weeks as neighbors got to the task at different times.

At first glance, the entire scene seemed to embody all the wholesomeness of a 1950s reading primer. Such books increased the budding student's vocabulary while reinforcing a picture of an idealized (if not idyllic) American way of life. "Dad" and "Mom," together with their children, "Dick" and "Jane" (and perhaps "Spot," the frisky family dog), happily cooperated in the familial enterprise. The primer would reformulate the celebration of healthy work and a well-ordered environment into a staccato of minimally complex sentences: "See Dad rake." "Dick and Jane are raking too." "Here comes mom!"

Since my parents were peasants from a Macedonian village, my family never quite fit this particular mold – especially when my mother would speak to me in Macedonian in front of my friends. Nonetheless, I distinctly remember teaching my illiterate mother to read from those very "Dick and Jane" primers so she could obtain her American citizenship, which she proudly accomplished in due time.

Before getting too nostalgic, however, let me remind you that all of this was taking place at the height of Cold War anxiety. Air-raid drills in our school, meant to prepare us and protect us from a Soviet nuclear strike, were another clear memory from my youth. (Nikita Khrushchev's shoe-banging incident at the United Nations in 1960 – together with his ominous and infamous greeting "We will bury you!" – captured the mood of this period.) The air-raid drills were carried out with due solemnity and seriousness – straight lines and no talking allowed. We would wind our way down into an elaborate, labyrinthine series of basement stories that had been constructed with the hopeless task of saving us from nuclear bombs. There we would sit in orderly rows, apparently oblivious to the real dangers of the Cold War world, until the all-clear signal indicated we could file back to our classrooms. Thus did the specter of the mushroom cloud darken the sunny skies of Dick and Jane's age of innocence.

And yet, beauty can be found even in the direst conditions. This time of year, I am often reminded of the remarkable akathist hymn, "Glory to God for All Things." Attributed to Metropolitan Tryphon (Prince Boris Petrovich Turkestanov, † 1934) it was later found among the remaining possessions of Protopresbyter Gregory Petrov († 1940). In unscientific (yet theologically poetic) imagery, he reminds us of God's glorious creation:

> O Lord, how lovely it is to be Your guest. Breeze full of scents; mountains reaching to the skies; waters like boundless mirrors, reflecting the sun's golden rays and the scudding clouds. All nature murmurs mysteriously, breathing the depth of tenderness. Birds and beasts of the forest bear the imprint of Your love. Blessed are you, mother earth, in your fleeting loveliness, which wakens our yearning for happiness that will last forever. In the land where, amid beauty that grows not old, rings out the cry: Alleluia! (*Kontakion* 2)

> You have brought me into life as if into an enchanted paradise. We have seen the sky like a chalice of deepest blue, where in the azure heights the birds are singing. We have listened to the soothing murmur of the forest and the melodious music of the streams. We have tasted fruit of fine flavor and the sweet-scented honey. We can live very well on Your earth. It is a pleasure to be Your guest. (*Ikos* 2)

> I see Your heavens resplendent with stars. How glorious You are, radiant with light! Eternity watches me by the rays of the distant stars. I am small, insignificant, but the Lord is at my side. Your right arm guides me wherever I go. (*Ikos* 5)

One wonders if the author of these words would have remained blind to all this beauty had he been "free," as we are, to be preoccupied with daily concerns that leave little opportunity to look around in awe? It recalls Dostoevsky's enigmatic phrase: "Beauty will save the world."

The First Monday of October
Originally Written: October 2016

"Let Us Attend!"

Take heed then to how you hear. (Lk 18.18)

Make sure that you never refuse to listen when He speaks. (Heb 12.25)

We are blessed with hearing the Scriptures at every Divine Liturgy. Whether the Liturgy is celebrated on the Lord's Day or on any other day of the week, we hear at least one reading from an Epistle and a Gospel. When the calendar so designates it, there may be two sets of readings – when there exists a complicated convergence of feast days and commemorations, there may even be as many as three prescribed readings. Whatever the case, these readings signify the culminating moments of the first part of the Liturgy, referred to as the "Liturgy of the Word," or "The Liturgy of the Catechumens." Before we commune with Christ in the Eucharist, we commune with Him through the inspired words of the Holy Scriptures – the *words* of the *Word*. This is the public proclamation of the word of God, meant to complement each believer's personal or domestic reading of the Scriptures. Just as we pray both liturgically and personally, so we read and listen to the Scriptures both liturgically and personally. Each is essential to support and make the other meaningful. To ignore one or the other is to impoverish our relationship with Christ.

By the presence of the Holy Spirit, our minds are open to the full meaning of the sacred texts that we hear. This was revealed to all Christians of all generations on the road to Emmaus, when the risen Lord encountered Cleopas and an unknown disciple: "And beginning with Moses and all the prophets, he interpreted to them in all the Scriptures the things concerning himself" (Lk 24.27). Following this encounter and the "breaking of the bread," during which these disciples recognized the risen Lord, "They said to each other, 'Did not our hearts burn within us while he talked to us on the road, while he opened to us the Scriptures?'" (Lk 24.32). Christ speaks to us today through the reading of the Scriptures, thus making it possible for us *today* to experience the identical "burning of heart" when we, too, make the time to read the Scriptures. As Fr John Behr succinctly said, "In the Church, we are still on the road to Emmaus."*

Due to the great importance of the liturgical proclamation of the Scriptures, these readings are prefaced by a dialog between the celebrant, the designated reader and the gathered faithful. I am specifically addressing the liturgical reading from the Gospel, aware that the preparation for the Epistle also has its own solemn and very similar introduction. Before the reading from the Gospel, we thus always hear:

> Priest or Deacon: Wisdom! Let us stand aright. Let us listen to the Holy Gospel.
>
> Bishop or Priest: Peace be unto all.
>
> People: And to your spirit.
>
> Priest or Deacon: The reading from the Holy Gospel according to St _____.
>
> People: Glory to Thee, O Lord, glory to Thee.
>
> Priest: Let us attend!

This solemn exchange is meant to get our attention – we are about to do something of great importance. The final words before the actual reading ("Let us attend!") are in some translations expressed with the phrase "Let us be attentive!" In informal English, this line

---

* John Behr, *Becoming Human: Meditations on Christian Anthropology in Word and Image* (Crestwood, NY: St Vladimir's Seminary Press, 2013), 15.

could be rendered even more simply: "Pay attention!" Immediately prior to this, we are directed to "stand aright." The distinction between these two commands is lost in some translations that employ the same English wording ("Let us attend") for both. In the original Greek, however, these are two separate directives. The first "Let us attend" is based on the Greek imperative *orthi*, which means to stand aright. The second "Let us attend!" comes from the Greek word *proskhomen,* which is an imperative to be attentive. Standing at attention, it seems, helps us gather our scattered thoughts better than sitting might. Standing is also a more reverent posture, appropriate for listening to the Lord's teaching through the words of the Gospel. Strange as it may sound to us, there is something of the soldier standing at solemn attention as he is about to hear his "orders" that must be faithfully fulfilled. This image is found often in Christian antiquity. In our Liturgy today, it is still a time when there should be no movement in the church – nothing to distract us from hearing the Gospel with an attentiveness that expresses our love of the Gospel as the "precious pearl" worth more than anything else. An outer silence in the church will hopefully facilitate an inner stillness within our minds and hearts that honors the Gospel reading as the sharing of the "words of eternal life."

As a possible test to measure our actual attentiveness at a given Liturgy, we can ask ourselves later in the day – or perhaps even during the week – what was the Gospel reading that I heard earlier in the Liturgy? Intently listening to the Gospel would mean that we can identify the evangelist and, even more importantly, the prescribed text(s) for the day. And the same should hold true for the Epistle reading. "He who has ears to hear, let him hear!" (Mt 11.15). If our ultimate goal is to live out the teachings of the Gospel, then we must meditate on the text with the goal of actualizing the teaching in our daily lives. How can we do this if we forget the Gospel reading once we leave the church? (The homily is meant to support that process, but that may or may not happen.) If we neglect to recall the Gospel reading, that means that we may have "attended" church, but that we were not "attentive" in church. To "be" in the Liturgy cannot be reduced to our bodily presence.

To further emphasize the great significance of the Gospel reading at the Liturgy, the celebrant offers a wonderful prayer before the dialog outlined above. Placed immediately after the final Alleluia verse following the Epistle reading, the prayer prepares us for the ensuing dialog. For this reason alone, it is my humble opinion that this "Prayer before the Gospel" should be chanted aloud by the celebrant of the Liturgy – the bishop or priest. Further, for the attentive reader of the Scriptures, there are numerous scriptural passages that are alluded to or paraphrased in this prayer, a few of which will be pointed out:

> Illumine our hearts [2 Cor 4.6], O Master Who lovest mankind, with the pure light [Rev 21.23–25] of Thy divine knowledge. Open the eyes of our mind [Eph 1.18; Lk 24.45] to the understanding of Thy Gospel teachings. Implant also in us the fear of Thy blessed commandments, that trampling down carnal desires [2 Pet 2.10], we may enter upon a spiritual manner of living [1 Cor 2.12], both thinking and doing such things as are well-pleasing unto Thee [Phil 2.13]. For Thou art the illumination of our souls and bodies, O Christ our God, and unto Thee we ascribe glory, together with Thy Father, who is from everlasting, and Thine all-holy, good, and life-creating Spirit, now and ever and unto ages of ages. Amen.

The Gospel reading occupies a prominent place during each Liturgy, because the Gospel is "good news" to which we should listen attentively – and *obey*. Familiarity may dull our appreciation of this, but when (over-)familiarity turns to boredom, then we are facing a spiritual crisis of sorts. We must always struggle against spiritual laziness or inattentiveness. Let us acknowledge how privileged and blessed we are to "stand aright" in church at the Liturgy and to hear the Holy Gospel. "Let us attend!"

The Second Monday of October
Originally Written: July 2009

Tribulation in This Life

At the moment our parish prayer request list is filled – as it often is – with the names of individuals in some condition of illness, suffering, or loss. We have been praying, for example, for a beloved child in our parish who has been in the hospital with pneumonia, as well as for another child in our sister parish who appears to have been born with a potentially fatal illness. Such prayer lists are by nature a sustained chronicle of the human suffering and misery we pray and hope to avoid. As we supplicate God for relief and recovery from the flesh-and-blood manifestations of our human condition, we fulfill a ministry that all Christians need to embrace with seriousness. Our task is to hold these persons before God in prayer – in the end, we leave the results up to God. It is only human to pray with greater intensity when a person in need of prayer is close to us, yet we also need to pray for everyone who is on our list, as the names come to us. That is one of our roles as the people of God, living in a world that is both fallen and yet has been redeemed by Christ.

I am not going to embark on a meditation concerning God's mercy, justice, and love in the face of human suffering – "theodicy," as it is called among philosophers. That will always remain a mystery. However, we should always bear in mind that the New Testament does not promise an end to the kind of suffering our prayer lists contain. There is no bargain to strike with God, no deal that grants us a long and prosperous life in return for our faith and belief in Christ. Although such a promise may exist in the minds of television evangelists and so-called "name-it-and-claim-it" preachers, it is found nowhere in the Scriptures. Christians with a mature faith know better. (On a side note: we of course believe in the possibility of miraculous recoveries, and have countless instances of such healing throughout the Church's long history. In fact, the sacrament of anointing is based on our openness to just such a possibility. Miracles such as these, are a different issue, however, and hearken back to the mystery of God's mercy mentioned above.)

Jesus Christ suffered and died on the cross. His resurrection from the dead transformed suffering into a passage that leads to a transformed life with God. As the Lord, He is the "first fruits" of that promised resurrection and glorified life (cf. 1 Cor 15.23). That is the hope of Christians in the face of suffering and death, both of which are inevitable. And that is a hope that unbelievers cannot share regardless of how optimistic they may be about life. We may realize this hope here and now in the recovery we pray for, or we may have to await its eschatological fulfillment at the end of time.

To move this reflection from the general to the particular, I find myself pondering a recent experience. Last week, Presvytera Deborah submitted a tender prayer request: "Please pray for Juana, a young beggar girl we encountered in Antigua who has no hands or feet. Pressing on my heart." Her words recalled our short and unsettling encounter with this little girl, whom we met on the last day of our most recent mission trip to Guatemala, on a one-day excursion to the capital of Antigua. The outing provided our team a chance to relax after a week of work at the Hogar Rafael Ayau Orthodox Orphanage.* Antigua is an old Guatemalan city popular with visitors and tourists, and our trip there was a kindness organized by the Hogar. In keeping with the "tradition" of the many teams our parish has brought over the years, we visited one of the fine restaurants in Antigua for a communal meal.

* This was the name of the refuge at the time this meditation was written. Today, the name of this mission is the Children's Orthodox Residence of San Miguel del Lago–Rafael Ayau.

While in the restaurant, I noticed a young girl – visibly impoverished – enter with a large purse. She appeared to have been ten years old or so. To my sadness, one of her arms was missing from just below the elbow – she held her purse at her elbow joint. A fuller glance revealed that both arms were missing at about the same point. As she moved from table to table with a rather awkward gait, it became clear that the girl had entered the restaurant to beg. (During her time in the restaurant, someone also noticed that she walked in a peculiar manner because she had no feet. There was instead a rather primitive contraption at the end of each leg resembling a shoe that helped her maintain her balance.) The relative indifference of the other patrons toward this young girl's presence indicated she was not a very unusual sight.

How differently this stark situation would have played out in the United States, where restaurant management "protects" its patrons from such an encounter by prohibiting begging. Indeed, I realized that this same girl may come often to this restaurant to seek alms, and that reality seemed organic and honest. It breaks down some of the usual social stratification to which we are accustomed. Nonetheless, since our social and cultural setting did shelter us in that instance, the encounter proved unsettling for our team. It was impossible not to feel great pity for this girl. Unfortunately, though, it appeared from my perspective that she was not very successful that day. Christ taught us that our left hand should not know what our right hand is doing in terms of almsgiving (Mt 6.3–4). I do not want to violate the Lord's teaching, but neither do I want you to think we ignored this poor little girl's need. As we called her over and deposited something in her purse, Presvytera Deborah asked her name. The girl answered with a warm and friendly smile, "Juana." That smile alone rendered rather feeble the tendency to assess quality of life with economic or other external measures. Joy still evident on her face, Juana turned and left the restaurant. We will probably never see her again, but she left an indelible and haunting image. She is a unique person and child of God who will not be forgotten in prayer.

Juana is also representative of the flawed and fallen world we inhabit. Yet she, and the world as it is, are the recipients of God's continuing love. That love – incarnate in Christ – does not make suffering disappear, but transforms its meaning. The task of Christians in this world is to continuously incarnate that love in their care for others, making Christ present in a tangible manner whenever called upon to do so. One way of incarnating love in this world is to pray for all persons on our "list" – whether they, or their form of suffering, is familiar to us or not. To pray is to remember living, human persons before God, and it is one way we make ourselves present not only to the love of God, but also to the suffering of others. In doing so, we actualize the love of God toward his children. That may be the most convincing "proof" of Christ's presence among us as a living reality, and not just as an ideal from the past.

The Third Monday of October
Originally Written: October 2015

"God or Nothing"

Recently, while browsing a bookstore, I was immediately attracted to the title of a new book *God or Nothing*, by Roman Catholic Cardinal Deacon Robert Sarah.[*] Although I have not actually read Cardinal Sarah's work, I would like to reflect on what I believe the title is alluding to, or what direction I would pursue were I the one writing a book with such a title. This is because I have concluded that if God exists, then we are "something." However, if God does not exist, then we are "nothing." Hence, my affinity for the starkness of this book's title – *God or Nothing*. This stark contrast is not meant to devalue genuine human experiences. On the contrary, as human beings we think and feel, we create and love, and these are only a few of the deep experiences that engender both joy and sorrow in life. Whether one identifies as a theist or an atheist, we all share these experiences, and they endlessly enrich our lives. Indeed, without them, life would essentially not be worth living.

Yet what is above, below, or behind such meaningful experiences? If God does not exist, then the inescapable (and, in my opinion, troubling) answer is nothing – literally. There only exists the void from which we emerged and to which we will return – there is life, then there is decay and death. This process of descent back into that void can be postponed but never eluded. The business of living life only disguises this stark truth, which is probably a good thing, otherwise there would be too much despair in the world.

[*] Cardinal Robert Sarah and Nicholas Diat, *God or Nothing: A Conversation on Faith with Nicholas Diat*, trans. Michael J. Miller (San Francisco, CA: Ignatius Press, 2015).

Nonetheless, I am trying to capture this wider-ranging aspect of our existence when I claim that if God is non-existent, then we are "nothing." And, of course, there is Dostoevsky's famous aphorism found throughout his masterpiece *The Brothers Karamazov*: "If God does not exist, then everything is permissible."

Yet if God does indeed exist – as we believe, proclaim, and hopefully live by – then we are genuinely "something." We do not hover in a void, but rather our lives are grounded in the ultimate reality. There is permanence above, below, and behind the world's transience – our lives count. Furthermore, they endure beyond the ravages of time and its attendant decay and death. That is because our lives are all contained within the "memory" of God. (Therefore, it is customary in the Orthodox Church to sing "Memory Eternal" for the departed.)

This "something" that we are if God exists is contained in that inexhaustible scriptural revelation that we are created in the image and likeness of God (cf. Gen 1.26). Our human capacity to think, feel, create, and love is the result of that wonderful truth – that God is the source and origin of our lives. It is because of Him we emerged from non-existence into being, which we receive as a gift to receive with thanksgiving. For this reason, we do not have to justify our intuitive capacity to seek moral, ethical, and spiritual truth. It is "natural" to be that way, because this conforms to the creative will of God. The tasks of life may distract us – at times even overwhelm us, but this "living life" (to borrow another phrase from Dostoevsky) signifies something and not nothing. Even further, if God *is*, then our lives add up to something much greater than the sum of all our human experiences in this life. The Gospel would call this "abundant" or "eternal" life (Jn 3.16, 10.10).

God or Nothing. All in all, an intriguing title for a book. I'm not sure I will ever read it, but for one last time I will claim that although stark, this either/or approach is vital – it reflects a deep look at reality. Could we even speak of a so-called middle choice? The agnostic "maybe" or "perhaps" does not sound very satisfying or reassuring. If we have chosen God over nothing, then our vocation is to embody this choice in lives that are full of meaningful pursuits, beginning with the God and Father of our Lord, Jesus Christ.

The Fourth Monday of October
Originally Written: October 2014

Moving beyond Mere Belief

Yet another bookstore-browsing session led me this time to the book review section of a religious journal, the name of which now escapes me. What does remain with me rather vividly is an intriguing quotation that kept coming to mind as I drove home afterwards:

I knew that you existed but did not believe it was so real.

Before I learned where this line originated, I assumed its anonymous author was from modernity. The words reminded me in some ways of C. S. Lewis's autobiographical work, *Surprised by Joy*, in which he describes his slow conversion to Christianity.[*] The quotation above also recalled the seventeenth-century French philosopher, Blaise Pascal, who wrote in his *Pensées* – in which he records his own conversion experience to a new and deeper faith – that he had encountered "not the God of the philosophers, but the God of Abraham, the God of Isaac and the God of Jacob."

Surprisingly, however, the text came from the wall of a church near some famous catacombs outside Rome (I believe those of Sts Callistus and Sebastian). That would place it somewhere in the second or third century of the Christian Era, yet its sentiment embodies what Archbishop Kallistos Ware wrote in his classic, *The Orthodox Way*:

> To believe in God is not to accept the possibility of his existence because it has been 'proved' to us by some

---

[*] C.S. Lewis, *Surprised by Joy: The Shape of My Early Life* (London, UK: William Collins, 1955).

theoretical argument, but it is to put our trust in One whom we know and love. Faith is not the supposition that something might be true, but the assurance the someone is there.[*]

Returning to the "so real" of the early Christian catacomb graffiti that so caught my attention, I believe that this phrase perfectly captures what today's world is so desperately looking for. This is a truly remarkable piece of graffiti – it says more in one brief sentence than some long and laborious theology books manage to communicate. A more contemporary observation reinforces that thought:

> The believer is not content with thinking of the world as created by a transcendent first cause; in the act of faith he cleaves to God himself, he addresses him directly, opens his heart to him as to an absolute Thou, in the hope that God will be his light, his truth and his life.[**]

Whoever scratched these words into that catacomb wall had an experience of the overwhelming and awesome presence of God, wherein God is no longer simply a concept or even an object of belief, but a living presence that almost takes one's breath away. This is the image of God that Jesus presented in His teachings – a God who was "so real," as the quotation puts it, that He could be called our Father. For only a God who was "so real" would number the hairs on our head (cf. Mt 10.30). With an experience like that of our anonymous wall-scribbler, we can then understand the teaching of Christ about leaving everything aside to continue that relationship, to which nothing can really compare. A God this real is "not the kind you have to wind up on Sunday," to quote a Jethro Tull song.

If we can manage to "lay aside all earthly cares," as the *Cherubic Hymn* admonishes, then perhaps such an experience of God is not

---

[*] (Crestwood, NY: St Vladimir's Seminary Press, 1979), 19.
[**] Matthew Levering, *Proofs of God: Classical Arguments from Tertullian to Barth* (Grand Rapids, MI: Baker Publishing Group, 2016), 23.

beyond our grasp. Our common hope as Christians is to move beyond the belief that God simply exists and into a true relationship with the living God, "who desires all men to be saved and to come to the knowledge of the truth" (1 Tim 2.4).

The First Monday of November
Originally Written: December 2007

Eucharistic Beings in a Eucharistic Society

In reading the account of Christ healing the ten lepers in the Gospel of St Luke, we learn how only one leper – a Samaritan at that – returned to Him to offer thanks: "Then one of them, when he saw that he was healed, turned back, praising God with a loud voice; and he fell on his face at Jesus' feet, giving him thanks. Now he was a Samaritan." This prompted Jesus' question: "Were not ten cleansed? Where are the nine? Was no one found to return and give praise to God except this foreigner?" (Lk 17.11–19). In this narrative, along with the miracle of healing, we encounter what is perhaps even more significant: the centrality of thanksgiving in one's relationship with God. Although they may have enjoyed their newly found good health, the nine lepers who failed to return to Christ to give thanks for their healing likely remained too self-absorbed to realize the true nature of healing. In failing to do so, they rendered their experience of healing incomplete, i.e., less thorough or "holistic" as Christ had intended.

To clarify, in no way was Jesus being petulant or making a self-centered demand for His "deserved" thanksgiving – He does not need such a response to satisfy any interior motivations or hidden agendas. Rather, His sole concern was that His heavenly Father be glorified for His great mercy and acknowledged as the source of all that is good. Christ wants us to manifest our "eucharistic" nature, so often obscured by a self-generated sinfulness that leaves us "missing the mark," the meaning of the Greek word for sin (*amartia*). The nine non-eucharistic lepers provide a stark example of precisely "missing the mark" by failing to respond to God with thanksgiving and love. Their encounter with the Father through Christ was lacking the synergy that harmoniously unites divine grace and human freedom in the process of salvation. Thus, we could raise an important question: although the nine lepers were "healed," were they "saved" as the Samaritan was?

The Greek term for thanksgiving (*eucharistia*) is related to the word for Eucharist. To be thankful is thus to encounter a profoundly biblical reality: "O give thanks unto the LORD, for he is good" (Ps 136.1). This is just as dominant a theme in the New Testament as in the Old: "I thank thee, Father, Lord of heaven and earth" (Mt 11.25). The frequency with which thankfulness is practiced throughout the Scriptures illustrates just how thoroughly we ought to regard the role of thanksgiving in our lives as Christians. Building on this necessity, there are three interrelated principles we can use to spur on thanksgiving in our lives.

1) We are "eucharistic beings." Created according to the image and likeness of God, we receive our lives and all that is in the world around us as a gift from our Creator. We are not self-sufficient beings, but dependent upon God for all things. We are fully human when we are *eucharistic*, when we offer thanksgiving to God in a spirit of humility and gratitude. Thus, it belongs to our deepest human nature – our very interior structure – to be eucharistic. A non-eucharistic person is dehumanized in the process.

2) We belong to a "eucharistic society." This is one more way of describing the Church. It is as members of the Body of Christ that we fulfill our role as eucharistic beings who live with a constant sense of thanksgiving and gratitude. The Church supports the world, and is the "place" within the world where the eucharistic dimension of our humanity is expressed on behalf of the entire world and creation: "Thine own of Thine own we offer unto Thee on behalf of all, and for all," as the prayer before the Anaphora reads *(Liturgy of St John Chrysostom)*. This same offering is made with a deep sense of thanksgiving. For it is within the Church that we respond with faith to the ultimate Gift of God – Jesus Christ, the Savior of the world. If the world fails in its vocation to be eucharistic, we continue to uphold the world precisely by being eucharistic.

3) We receive the Eucharist. Here, the term *Eucharist* refers to the very body and blood of Christ, or Holy Communion, as we also call it. The Divine Liturgy can be called the eucharistic service of the Church, during which we receive the Eucharist after thanking God for the entire economy of our salvation: "And we thank Thee for this Liturgy which Thou hast deigned to accept at our hands." Ideally, at least, we should not arrive at church for the Liturgy with a sense of religious obligation, but with a deep sense of thanksgiving before our awesome God, who has done everything possible to endow us with His Kingdom that is to come. Unworthy though we may be, God has made us worthy to receive the Eucharist as a foretaste of the heavenly banquet in His eternal Kingdom.

As human beings – and more specifically as Christians – we have a common vocation as eucharistic beings who belong to a eucharistic society, and who receive the Eucharist as a gift of grace. For this, we are profoundly thankful to God.

The Second Monday of November
Originally Written: November 2012

Forty Shopping (and Fasting) Days until Christmas

November 15 commences the forty-day Nativity Fast, meant to prepare us for the advent of the Son of God in the flesh. For many of us, this might catch us unaware and unprepared. Nonetheless, "it is what it is," as the saying goes, and the Church calendar continues to direct us into this sacred season. This indicates an intensification of the perennial "battle of the calendars" mentioned earlier. This is a struggle every Orthodox Christian is engaged in, whether consciously or unconsciously – the two calendars, the ecclesial and the secular, represent the Church and the world, respectively.

Because of the tension between the two, we often find ourselves in the peculiar situation of being *ascetic* and *consumerist* simultaneously. In the context of our contemporary world, to be ascetic means to live more simply. This requires a commitment to self-discipline, which we can learn through the traditional Christian efforts of fasting, praying, and practicing charity. Cultivating simplicity requires both intentional discipline and a conscious desire to live by the principles of the Gospel in a highly secularized and increasingly hedonistic world. To be an ascetic is not to be a fanatic, but to follow the words of Christ who taught us to practice "self-denial" (Mk 8.34). It further means to focus our lives on Christ amid an ever-increasing number of distractions and diversions. That is hardly an easy endeavor, even with the best of intentions. In an age when everything we could want or need is readily available to us, voluntary self-restraint is tantamount to dying to the world. Such efforts are nothing short of offering a genuine Christian witness to the world.

While the Church invites us into ascetic moderation, however, our society beckons us into consumerism, counting down the remaining shopping days until Christmas. Spending money is an almost patriotic act of contributing to the revitalization of our failing economy. Nevertheless, is it really a comfort when the nightly news informs us that consumer retail spending rose 3.5% from the previous year? Why conflate the saving economy (*oikonomia*) of the Son of God with the fortunes of the economy?

It is human to want to fit in – especially for the sake of our children – but we risk unleashing the "consumer within," who lives for the joys of shopping, spending, and accumulating. Add to this the unending entertainments designed to create a festive holiday atmosphere and it can all become rather overwhelming. Certainly, this time of year contributes to the joys of family life, and surrounding our children with the warmth of gift giving brings a sense of security to our domestic lives. Perhaps, though, we can be vigilant and discern when "enough is enough," or rather: when "enough is a feast." Being aware – and generous toward – those who have next to nothing is another way of overcoming our own self-absorption and expanding our notion of the "neighbor."

Bearing all of this in mind, the struggle for asceticism lies at the heart of our challenge to be Christians in a world that caters to our consumerist tendencies. To speak honestly, this is a difficult and uneasy balance to maintain. I believe what is at stake is not simply our checkbooks or spending habits, but our central identity as Orthodox Christians within the confines of a culture either indifferent or hostile to Christianity. If the Church remains an essential part of our preparation for Christmas, we can progress toward balancing a (hopefully moderate) level of unavoidable consumerism with asceticism. If our life in the Church at the very least "competes" with the lure of the mall – in terms of our time, energy, and concern – that is a small victory in the larger, lifelong battle for our ultimately loyalty. The Church directs us to fast before we feast. Does that make any sense? Do we understand the theological/spiritual principles that are behind such an approach? Can we develop some domestic strategies that will give us the opportunity to put that into practice, at least to some extent? Do we even care?

The final question always returns us to the question that Jesus asked of His initial disciples: "Who do you say that I am?" (cf. Mk 8.27). If we, together with St Peter, confess that Jesus is "the Christ, the Son of the Living God," then we know where we stand as the battle of the calendars intensifies over the next forty days. In such a way, these forty days will result in a meaningful journey toward the mystery of the incarnation rather than in an exhaustive excursion toward a vapid winter holiday. The choice is ours to make.

The Third Monday of November
Originally Written: November 2015

Indulging Not in Food, But in Giving Thanks to the Lord

A few years ago, I ran across an op-ed piece in the newspaper titled "A Moveable Fast," by Elyssa East.* Such a title in a well-known urban secular publication caught my eye, especially since the article's concluding paragraph can be read in an "Orthodox manner" without a great deal of manipulation:

> In the nearly 400 years since the first Thanksgiving, the holiday has come to mirror our transformation into a nation of gross overconsumption, but the New England colonists never intended for Thanksgiving to be a day of gluttony. They dished up restraint along with gratitude as a shared main course. What mattered most was not the feast itself, but the gathering together in thanks and praise for life's most humble gifts. Perhaps this holiday season we could benefit from restoring a proper Thanksgiving balance between forbearance and indulgence.

In other words, the uneasy alliance that has formed over the years between Thanksgiving and indulgence does not properly capture the meaning of this national holiday. For Thanksgiving to be properly "observed," a "gathering together in thanks and praise" is the most appropriate response. This is a good, albeit brief, definition of what we do in the Divine Liturgy. The Eucharist is about our thanksgiving to God – not only for what we may have, but for who we *are* and are becoming as the people of God, growing into His likeness through Christ and the gift of the Holy Spirit. We celebrate that service of thanksgiving – the Eucharist – so

* *New York Times*, Nov. 23, 2009.

that we may realize our vocation as "eucharistic beings," and not as mere "consumers." For those who like theological jargon, our anthropology is maximalist, not minimalist. Just as we engage in the festal Thanksgiving Day table in our homes, we continually make the effort to receive the eucharistic food from the altar table in a spirit of praise and thanksgiving. And we do so joyfully and eagerly.

Elyssa East's op-ed article includes a fascinating historical sketch of the mind and practices of the early Puritans in seventeenth-century New England. Fasting and feasting were part of their way of life. Admittedly, I would acknowledge that the "Orthodox ethos" and the "Puritan ethos" are as far apart as one could imagine. There is the saying that a Puritan is a person who is afraid that someone, somewhere, and for some reason is actually enjoying himself. The Calvinist notion of an angry God who needs to be appeased before He unleashes His punishment does not resonate with Orthodox theology – and we thank our merciful God for that. Perhaps the harsh environment and struggle for survival experienced by these early Puritans further influenced some of their bleak theological conclusions. Aside from this, however, some practices adopted by the Puritans may coincide with those of Orthodoxy. The author relates, for example, that the Puritans' fear of "excessive rains from the bottles of heaven," and "epidemics, crop infestations, the Indian wars and other hardships," led them to call for community-wide days of fasting or a "day of public humiliation and prayer." She further writes:

> According to the nineteenth-century historian William DeLove, the New England colonies celebrated as many as nine such "special public days" a year from 1620-1700. And as the Puritans were masters of self-denial, days of abstention outnumbered thanksgivings two to one. Fasting, Cotton Mather wrote, "kept the wheel of prayer in continual motion."

Our fasting as Orthodox Christians, however, is not based on a fearful notion of appeasing God; rather, it is a freely chosen ascetical effort of self-discipline that seeks to actualize the words of the Lord when He fasted in the desert: "Man shall not live by bread alone, but by every word that proceeds from the mouth of God" (Mt 4.4). The rhythm of fasting and feasting is directed by our liturgical calendar, as we are now fasting in preparation for the Feast of the Nativity. We are, however, granted a hierarchical "dispensation" on Thanksgiving Day to "break the fast" so we may celebrate this national holiday as Americans. Actually, the Orthodox can hold their own with any other religiously based culture when it comes to feasting. We have a great deal to feast about when we reflect upon the divine economy, yet even feasting is not about "gross overconsumption" and mere indulgence.

A few more of Elyssa East's paragraphs help us understand the historical, cultural and religious background of our Thanksgiving Day celebration. "It was in the late 1660s that the New England colonies began holding an 'Annual Provincial Thanksgiving,'" she writes:

> The holiday we celebrate today is a remnant of this harvest feast, which was theologically counterbalanced by an annual spring fast around the time of planting to ask God's good favor for the year. Yet fasting and praying also immediately preceded the harvest Thanksgiving. In 1690, in Massachusetts the feast itself was postponed, though not the fasting, out of extraordinary concern that the meal would inspire too much "carnal confidence." As life in the New World wilderness got easier, the New England colonies gradually began holding only their annual spring fast and fall harvest feast. Even after Abraham Lincoln established Thanksgiving as a national holiday in 1863, Massachusetts continued to celebrate its spring day of abstention for 31 more years.

As "right believing" Christians, we know to whom we offer our thanksgiving and why – not only on Thanksgiving Day, but at every eucharistic Divine Liturgy. As the royal priesthood (see 1 Pet 2.5) of believers, it is our responsibility to hold up the world in prayer before God – Father, Son, and Holy Spirit. If this national holiday is now characterized by gross overconsumption, that does not mean that we need to follow such a pattern when we have the opportunity to thank and praise God before we partake of our domestic meals together. Perhaps a more theologically grounded understanding of "Eucharist" can lead us toward a Thanksgiving Day celebration that is as spiritually healthy as it is enjoyable to our senses.

The Fourth Monday of November
Originally Written: November 2004

Preparing for the Incarnation

On this Monday morning, we begin the second week of the Nativity Fast that prepares us for the feast of our Savior's birth in the flesh. Periodically, it is worthwhile to revisit the theme of preparation and waiting in our lives. Why prepare for Christmas with prayer, almsgiving, and fasting when we could easily join the world and "party" our way to December 25? It is, after all, an exceedingly merry season. "'Tis the season to be jolly," so why bother with ascetical effort? One wonders if, in observing the Nativity Fast, we prove ourselves unable to part with a tradition that has become largely meaningless aside from some old-world nostalgia.

To the contrary, however, this season of preparation reflects a profound historical and theological truth: it reveals how God himself acted within salvation history. He has moved slowly and providentially through time. Even within its schematic nature, Scripture leaves long intervals of time between the First and Last Adam. The long preparation experienced by the "Israel of God" was not yet the time for jubilation, but instead a season for prophecy and for waiting. The angelic revelation to the shepherds occurred only after Christ was born:

> And the angel said to them, 'Be not afraid; for behold, I bring you good news of a great joy which will come to all the people; for to you is born this day in the city of David a Savior, who is Christ the Lord.' (Lk 2.10–11)

This centuries-long period of waiting was characterized not only by "prayer and fasting," but by perseverance, faith and hope:

"And all these, though well attested by their faith, did not receive what was promised, since God had foreseen something better for us, that apart from us they should not be made perfect" (Heb 11.39–40).

In fact, the limits of human endurance were tested:

> Some were tortured, refusing to accept release, that they might rise again to a better life. Others suffered mocking and scourging, and even chains and imprisonment. They were stoned, they were sawn in two, they were killed with the sword; they went about in skins of sheep and goats, destitute, afflicted, ill-treated – of whom the world was not worthy – wandering over deserts and mountains, and in dens and caves of the earth. (Heb 11.35–38)

These passages are read in the Liturgy on the Sunday before Christmas. In this context, the Nativity's season of preparation is a type of Israel's waiting for the coming of the Messiah. Within the forty-day microcosm of Israel's history, we experience both waiting and expectation. Our modest ascetical effort is meant to re-actualize or make real and present in our lives the difficult and demanding experience of Israel. Our own disregard for the Church's prescribed disciplines during this season should be a source of repentance when we compare them to the great demands God made of His chosen people. This is especially true when we consider they were never certain when or even whether their hard-earned faith would be fulfilled.

From a historical perspective, I would venture that our present pre-Christmas whirl of shopping, spending, and partying emerged rather recently. The so-called "twelve days of Christmas" are the days following the Feast of the Nativity, which reflect the revealed joy of the birth of Christ. The traditional carol of that title is a playful reflection of the Church's liturgical calendar, both in the East and West. It is for this reason that the longest fast-free period in the Church occurs precisely from Christmas to the eve of Theophany (January 5), which is a strict fast day. Feasting follows fasting.

We live and experience the tension – not necessarily a gulf or absolute separation, but a tension nonetheless – between the Church and the world that exists in relation to the birth of Christ. An honest awareness of this tension is essential for us to make responsible decisions in the light of our faith in Christ. This also sets the tone for our families and affects our witness to the world. Perhaps a little "non-conformity" will yield its fruit in due season. The sheer exhaustion and the post-holiday blues that afflict many people are to some extent the result of draining the season of its inherent celebratory nature before Christmas even arrives. If we are not spiritually vigilant, we may do no more than drag our exhausted bodies and souls off to the Liturgy, which is supposed to be the joyful fulfillment of this wonderful season of preparation, reducing what the Typikon of the Church refers to as "a splendid three-day Pascha" into a period of convalescence. There is a great wisdom in the Church that we must never feel reluctant to draw upon – as the body of Christ and temple of the Holy Spirit, the Church will not let us down.

The First Monday of December
Originally Written: December 2007

The Image of Giving in St Nicholas

On December 6, we commemorate St Nicholas of Myra. A certain tension accompanies his person and memory. On the one hand, there are few undisputable facts about his life (to the point where many doubt his actual historical existence). On the other, St Nicholas is one of the most beloved and universally venerated saints within the Church – even many Muslims venerate him:

> Little is known for certain about the life of St Nicholas, bishop of Myra in Lycia (Asia Minor). It is believed that he suffered imprisonment during the last major persecution of the Church under Diocletian in the early fourth century, and that he attended the first Ecumenical Council at Nicaea in 325. Christian tradition has come to regard him, in the words of an Orthodox hymn, as "an example of faith and an icon of gentleness."[*]

For those interested in the historical background of St Nicholas, the following note is found in the *Synaxarion*:

> Since the medieval period, St Nicholas of Myra has been confused with St Nicholas of Sion, who founded a monastery not far from Myra at the end of the 5th century. The Vita of the latter has come down to us but the incidents in it have been entirely ascribed to St Nicholas of Myra, with the result that St Nicholas of Sion has been forgotten in the hagiographical accounts.[**]

---

[*] George Every, Richard Harries, and Kallistos Ware, *The Time of the Spirit* (Crestwood, NY: St Vladimir's Seminary Press, 1984), 69.
[**] *The Synaxarion: The Lives of the Saints of the Orthodox Church*, vol. 2 (Ormylia, Chakidike, Greece: The Annunciation of Our Lady, 1999), 332; cf. *The Life of*

Even if St Nicholas the Wonderworker is a composite figure, when we venerate him we are given a glimpse into the mind of the Church when it comes to an image of a true pastor. We find in the accounts of St Nicholas a powerful and enduring image of a genuine Christian shepherd, regardless of the now unrecoverable details of his true life. It is this "unerring" intuition of the people of God that upholds all the wonderful stories that endear us to St Nicholas. The Church today desperately needs bishops of the type embodied by St Nicholas. Such a bishop would – if sincerely embracing traditional virtues – inspire his flock far more than even a capable diocesan administrator.

> You appear to your flock as a rule of faith, an image of humility and a teacher of abstinence. Because of your lowliness Heaven was opened to you; because of your poverty riches were granted to you. O Holy Bishop Nicholas pray to Christ our God that our souls may be saved.
> (*Troparion of St Nicholas*)

St Nicholas both protected and interceded for his flock, according to the great Russian Orthodox iconographer, Leonid Uspensky.

> This "life for others" is [St Nicholas'] characteristic feature and is manifested by the great variety of forms of his solicitude for men: his care for their preservation, their protection from the elements, from human injustice, from heresies and so forth. This solicitude was accompanied by numerous miracles both during his life and after his death. Indefatigable intercessor, steadfast, uncompromising fighter for Orthodoxy, he was meek and gentle in character and humble in spirit.[*]

As famous as St Nicholas has been, he is perhaps less well-known in today's world. Santa Claus, that rather unfortunate caricature of

---

Saint Nicholas of Sion, ed. and trans. Ihor Sevcenko and Nancy Patterson (Brookline, MA: Hellenic College Press, 1984).
[*] Every, Harries, and Ware, *Time of the Spirit*, 69.

the saintly bishop, has something to do with this, but the very virtues embodied by this saint are slowly fading from our consciousness.

Perhaps the most enduring quality of the figure of St Nicholas is that of giving, particularly to children in need. Even at Christmastime, we often perpetuate the widening gap between the "haves" and "have-nots" without too many pangs of (Christian) conscience. St Nicholas wanted to restore a sense of balance, and looked first to those who were in need, giving them a taste of childlike happiness when they received an unexpected gift. In a simple manner, this imitates the giving of God, who gave us Christ at a time when everyone – rich and poor alike – was impoverished through sin and death.

I sometimes fantasize that an ideal celebration of Christmas would find a relatively affluent family making sure that they spent more on those in need than on themselves. If Christianity is indeed the "imitation of the divine nature," as St Gregory of Nyssa once said, then that is not an unrealistic idea. I do not believe that I have ever done that, so I convict myself through the very thought. Yet, I am convinced that our children would respond with an eager spirit of cooperation if properly prepared for a Christmas of giving rather than of getting. Is it not, as Christ said, more blessed to give than to receive (Acts 20.35)?

The Second Monday of December
Originally Written: December 2012

In the Fullness of Time

The epistle reading for the Feast of our Lord's Nativity is brief but powerful and profound in all its revealed implications:

> But when the time had fully come, God sent forth his Son, born of woman, born under the law, to redeem those who were under the law, so that we might receive adoption as sons. And because you are sons, God has sent the Spirit of his Son into our hearts, crying, "Abba! Father!" So through God you are no longer a slave but a son, and if a son then an heir. (Gal 4.4–7)

Here, the Apostle Paul affirms the incarnation of the Son of God – Jesus of Nazareth, the Messiah of Israel, and the Savior of the world. If God sent forth His Son, the Son must already have existed, or (to use a theological term) "pre-existed" as the eternal Son of the eternal Father prior to entering the world as a human being. The Son did not come into existence as a new person when He was "born of a woman." Rather the eternal Person of the Son now assumed our human nature and began to live as Jesus of Nazareth, "born under the law." That He was "born of a woman" affirms His true humanity, that Jesus is one of us. At the same time, being "born under the law" testifies to His unique role within Israel's messianic role among the nations.

The entrance hymn sung during the Vespers of the Nativity melds the theme of God's action through history with the glorification of the incarnation:

> When Augustus ruled alone upon the earth, the many kingdoms of men came to an end, and when Thou wast

> made man of the pure virgin, the many gods of idolatry were destroyed.
>
> The cities of the world passed under one single rule, and the nations came to believe in one sovereign Godhead.
>
> The peoples were enrolled by the decree of Caesar, and we the faithful were enrolled in the Name of the Godhead, when Thou, our God, wast made man.
>
> Great is Thy mercy, O Lord! Glory to Thee!

This magnificent hymn expands upon the account found in the Gospel according to St Luke of the historical conditions under which Christ entered the world: "In those days a decree went out from Caesar Augustus that all the world should be enrolled. This was the first enrollment, when Quirin'ius [*sic*] was governor of Syria" (Lk 2.1–2). Caesar Augustus was the first Roman emperor (27 BC-14 AD) and inaugurated the glory days of Rome during the early years of Christ's life. It is said that he inaugurated the *pax romana*, the Roman peace that supposedly made for a more stable and less militant world. Everything from Roman roads to Roman administration served the empire and the peaceful world it sought to protect and preserve. For this, Augustus was even called "Lord" and "Savior." This, of course, was a political conceit – it was Rome's military might that ruled the Mediterranean world, ruthlessly suppressing dissidence. Roman taxation and garrisons throughout the empire were oppressive rather than liberating. This was especially true in Israel, where the Roman presence was a cause of great anguish. How could Caesar rather than the Lord, who had expressed His will for the destiny of Israel by revealing the Law, rule the people of God?

It was into this world that the Son of God was incarnated. He was a king, but one who did not rule by coercion or military prowess. For His kingdom was that of God, and through His teaching the virtues implanted in the minds and hearts of human beings were meant to inwardly transform lives so that peace could radiate outward from its source: a repentant heart oriented toward God. In a somewhat polemical fashion, St Luke revealed to us the "real" Lord and Savior in the birth of Jesus of Nazareth. That event led us to calculate time differently. That Christ came in "the fullness of time" is much more than a chronological indication. It means that this was the chosen moment for God to act, and this "ripening" of time led us to calculate time based upon the advent of Christ in the flesh.

Our hearts should neither be directed to nor disillusioned by Augustus or whatever political power may rule: "Put not your trust in princes, in a son of man, in whom there is no help" (Ps 146.3). Rather, we should orient ourselves toward the mystery revealed in Bethlehem, when both the cosmos and the world – represented by angels and humble shepherds – joined together in praising and worshipping the newborn child wrapped in swaddling clothes. There is not a great deal of room left here for sentimentality and warm feelings. St Luke is articulating a historical theology that reminds us God acts within human history to redeem us from the horrors of sin and death. Ultimately, this child will offer His life on the cross for our salvation.

As we approach the festal date of December 25, I hope our hearts can focus on the mystery of the incarnation. If we plan appropriately, we can be sure that before all else, we are committed to be in church to worship Christ, the Son of God who entered the world "when the time had fully come" (Gal 4.4). The forty-day Nativity Fast culminates in the Lord's entrance into the world in the flesh. As Israel was prepared by God to receive its Messiah, we have been prepared within the Church to again actualize this mystery that was hidden before the ages but is now revealed to us in Christ. The festal Liturgy on the morning of December 25 needs to take precedence over our other warm family traditions that are meant to further fill our homes with the radiant presence of Christ. How can we properly celebrate Christmas without first being in church to worship the newborn Christ and receive the Eucharist? Our humble witness to the world is that we place Christ at the very heart of our lives – as families and as parishes.

The Third Monday of December
Originally Written: December 2010

Christmas and Martyrdom

The Gospel reading on the Feast of the Nativity of Our Lord is Matthew 2.1–12, a passage that proclaims the good news of the Savior's birth in Bethlehem. Following a rather laconic description of Christ's nativity, the evangelist Matthew turns to the drama between King Herod and the "wise men from the East" (Mt 2.1). We refer to these wise men as magi, based on the original Greek text. Guided by the star, they brought their gifts of gold, frankincense, and myrrh to the newborn child. In doing so, they acknowledged that He is the true king testified to by cosmic signs even the Gentiles could understand. Joyous as this event was, however, the infancy narratives in this Gospel also bear the shadow of the cross. Even on this blessed feast, we find in the Gospel reading a hint of Christ's ultimate destiny – myrrh was an oil used in Jewish burial customs. Thus, we find a clear anticipation of the Lord's death and burial.

On the day after the Nativity Feast, we read further in St Matthew's Gospel about the tragic massacre of the innocent boys in and around Bethlehem who were two years old or younger (2.16–18). The blood shed by these "holy innocents" was the result of a decree from King Herod, who perceived in Christ's birth a threat to his kingdom. Yesterday's joy over the Savior's nativity is now replaced by the wailing and lamentation of the mothers of these precious children. It was a scene that vividly fulfilled the prophetic words of Jeremiah more than half a millennium before the birth of Christ: "A voice was heard in Ramah, / wailing and loud lamentation, / Rachel weeping for her children; / she refused to be consoled, / because they were no more" (Mt 2.18; cf. Jer 31.15).

King Herod's paranoia seemed boundless – even members of his family were not protected from his murderous mistrust. As the aphorism attributed to the Roman Emperor Augustus reportedly said: "I would rather be Herod's pig than son."

In the immediate post-Nativity period, these male children represent the first of many martyrs who would die as a result of Christ entering the world. These early, innocent deaths are a sober reminder that Christ's birth cannot be reduced to a sentimental round of Christmas carols sung around the Christmas tree with cups of hot chocolate. The entrance of God's Son into the world was a jarring intrusion into the brokenness of human striving. As such, the dark example of King Herod foreshadows many of the powerful figures in this world who, instead of receiving Christ, have despised Him and turned against His followers. Nonetheless, the suffering of innocent children is somehow taken up by God as an offering in a sinful world that fluctuates between light and darkness. By their witness, we now more fully understand that the cave of the nativity anticipated the tomb of Christ's burial, and that the swaddling clothes anticipated the grave clothes that would eventually bind Christ following His death on the cross.

Finally, on the third day of the nativity, we commemorate the Protomartyr Stephen, the first to die for his faith in Christ in the post-resurrection Church. This martyrdom, together with the saint's compelling speech before the Jewish Council, was recorded in great detail and drama in Acts 6 and 7. This highly significant and even ominous event served to forewarn the Church of perilous events to come. The Savior's followers where not to live under the illusion that they were immune from the persecution that befell their master. Martyrdom has always been a distinct and powerful witness to Christ. The Kontakion of St Stephen captures the movement from the joy of Christ's birth to the sobering reality of what Christ's coming meant for some:

Yesterday the Master assumed our flesh and became our guest;
Today His servant is stoned to death and departs in the flesh:
The glorious first martyr Stephen!

There is no greater witness to Christ than that of the martyrs – flesh-and-blood men, women, and children who gave their lives for the Lord in the hope and assurance that eternal life awaited them. The Church believes and proclaims that the names of the martyrs are written in the Book of Life. Moreover, the earlier venerated saints of the Church were the holy martyrs, whose blood Tertullian described as "the seed of the Church." When we greet others with the words "Merry Christmas," we always need to be mindful of the commitment we are making to the newborn Christ. As we temporarily indulge in the days of the afterfeast – the longest fast-free period in the liturgical year – we ought to remember that the Christian life is ultimately a commitment to discipline and restraint. It is even a "crucifixion" of the flesh, with all its desires (cf. Gal 5.16–21). This will greatly strengthen our witness to Christ as disciples who believe that His advent in the flesh, culminating in His death and resurrection, will prepare a place for us in His eternal kingdom where there is "life everlasting."

The Fourth Monday of December
Originally Written: December 2012

The Incarnation: A Word about the Word

He, the Mighty One, the Artificer of all, Himself prepared this body in the virgin as a temple for Himself, and took it for His very own, as the instrument through which He was known and in which He dwelt.
– St Athanasius the Great, *On the Incarnation of the Word*

Within the Church, we have a biblical or theological vocabulary to express what we believe as Christians. These words are drawn primarily from the Bible, the ecumenical councils, and the theological writings of Church fathers like St Athanasius, quoted above. As responsible, practicing Christians, we need to know this vocabulary, at least in its most basic forms. Just as we continually learn the parlance of new technologies – from computers to smartphones – so too we ought to familiarize ourselves with the language of the Church as it has been sanctified over centuries of use. This vocabulary should be natural to us, like a mother tongue, not a manner of speaking that is foreign, exotic, or "only for theologians."

As we continue to celebrate the Nativity of our Lord Jesus Christ, a key term in our vocabulary as Orthodox Christians is incarnation – the birth of Christ was the *incarnation* of the Son of God. Turning to the dictionary, we find the term defined in a rather bland and truncated fashion, described simply as

in•car•na•tion \in-kär-`nā-shən\ *noun*

1 a: the embodiment of a deity or spirit in some earthly form.

> b: *capitalized:* the union of the divinity with humanity in Jesus Christ.[*]

In contrast to this rather terse explanation, Orthodox theologian Fr John Anthony McGuckin includes an extensive entry for this term in *The Westminster Handbook to Patristic Theology*. His definition begins as follows:

> Incarnation is the concept of the eternal Word of God (the *Logos*) "becoming flesh" within history for the *salvation* of the human race. Incarnation does not simply refer to the act itself (such as the conception of Jesus in the womb of the Virgin, or the event of Christmas); it stands more generally for the whole nexus of events in the life, teachings, sufferings, and glorification of the Lord, considered as the earthly, embodied activity of the Word.[**]

Speaking of expanding our theological vocabulary, we need to further know that we translate the key Greek term *Logos* as "Word," referring of course to the Word who was "with God" and who "was God," according to St John's Gospel "in the beginning" (Jn 1.1–2). We also refer to the Word of God as the "Son," "wisdom," and "power" of God. It is this Logos/Word of God who becomes incarnate as Jesus of Nazareth. The most defining expression of the incarnation in the New Testament is in the Gospel according to St John "And the *Word* [Logos] became flesh" (1.14, emphasis added). Incarnation is derived from the Latin word meaning "in the flesh." The Greek word for this would be *sarkothenta*, "made flesh." In other words, the incarnation of the Word of God is the "enfleshment" of the Word, flesh representing the totality of our human nature. The Word has assumed our human nature and united it to himself in an indissoluble way that restores the fellowship of God and humankind. The sacramental life of the Church is based on the incarnation, as is the potential for created reality to

---

[*] "Incarnation," Merriam Webster's Collegiate Dictionary, https://www.merriam-webster.com/dictionary/incarnation.
[**] (Louisville, KY: Westminster John Knox Press, 2004), 180.

become a vehicle for spiritual reality. The ultimate manifestation of sacramental reality is the Eucharist, in which the bread and wine become the body and blood of Christ.

Christmas is the time of the year to recall this profound reality and recover a genuine Christian vocabulary that expresses our faith in Christ, and what – through Him – humanity has the potential to become. When approached with reverence and wonder, these theological words are not dry and abstract concepts. They enliven the reading and studying of our theological tradition, and humble us in the process. The vocabulary of faith reveals life-transforming truths that, if received with prayer and thanksgiving, enhance and expand our minds and hearts, that we might have the "mind of Christ" (1 Cor 2.16).

The Fifth Monday of December
Originally Written: January 2009

The Time of Our Lives

As January 1 approaches, we find ourselves newly aware of the inexorable and irrepressible passage of time. Sweeping us along in its current, where is time carrying us? The very nature of time is difficult to grasp. Cosmically and geologically, we may measure it in terms of millions or even billions of years. Historically, we measure time in terms of millennia or centuries. On a personal level, we measure time in terms of decades, years, months, weeks, days, hours, minutes, and seconds. That is called chronological time.

But what of a more psychological or existential experience of time? The seemingly simple reality of time can leave us groping for an answer that fails to come readily. In Book XI of his *Confessions*, Blessed Augustine of Hippo († 430) brilliantly described the virtually universal struggle to grasp the very concept of time:

> What is time? Who can explain this easily and briefly? Who can comprehend this even in thought so as to articulate the answer in words? Yet what do we speak of, in our familiar everyday conversation, more than of time? We surely know what we mean when we speak of it. We also know what is meant when we hear someone else talking about it. What then is time? Provided that no one asks me, I know. If I want to explain it to an inquirer, I do not know.

We speak of time in terms of tenses – past, present, and future. However, do the past and the future truly exist? When the present becomes the past, does it still exist somehow? Moreover, what about the future – it eventually becomes the present, only to retreat into the past? How can even the present exist with any true substance, since it fades away the moment it appears? We quickly face some perplexing questions whenever we attempt to speak about time. Yet, as Augustine wrote, we all know what is meant by time, though we cannot articulate what it is we know.

I believe time is our most precious commodity. Time is life, because we live our lives within time. When, for us, there is no more time, there is consequently no more life, in the earthly sense. We speak of a dead person as no longer having any time – his time is up, in a manner of speaking. If we live within time, however, and if time is our most precious commodity in that life, why do we so often speak of "wasting time" – or worse: "killing time"? We waste time waiting in line at the grocery store checkout, or kill time between appointments or flights. What is it we are really wasting or killing – is it not life itself? Perhaps these idioms are now an inevitable and unavoidable linguistic development, but they do reflect something of the quotidian nature of our lives and of time itself.

A more beneficial picture of reality would involve filling up this precious time rather than wasting or killing it. Instead of becoming impatient with the person in the so-called express line who has thirteen items (instead of the maximum twelve), what if we filled that time with interior prayer, perhaps in the form of the Jesus Prayer? The same for driving, walking, or any other daily activity. With some effort and discipline, it is always possible to "redeem the time" (see Eph 5.16). (This endeavor, by the way, has nothing to do with merely keeping busy, which can become the greatest source of wasting and killing time imaginable. If we could become less busy, perhaps we would be better stewards of the time given to us.)

God has placed us within the time of the created world. Time is God's gift to us. A Christian acknowledges that time leads us to our deaths, but it also leads us to eternity. In a work entitled "Eternity and Time: Oration for the New Year," Fr Sergius Bulgakov beautifully expressed the Christian hope that time is not a meaningless movement toward a meaningless death:

> The gates of the future are open before us, and through them we pass from time to beyond time, into eternity. Earthly time will cease to be with our death, and especially with the death of the entire world, beyond which its transfiguration will take place. Time will cease to be when the Lord comes. To Him, to His coming to us, we are led by time. Time is woven into a knot at this point. It is that truly new thing for us – the new life, the new heaven and earth – for which we yearn.... And our New Year prayer contains, like the beating of the Christian heart, the Christian call and beckoning: "Even so, come Lord Jesus" [Rev 22.20].*

As trite as it sounds, come January 1, we will be nearly 365 days closer to that reality than our last New Year's celebration. For that reason, we need to think deeply about the direction our lives take through time. After all, we do not have an endless store of time – only God knows the amount allotted to each one of us. It is a gift we must not squander. An immediate challenge that the New Year will pose for us is expressed in one of the special petitions found in the prayer service for the New Year, which we offer up to God on an annual basis:

> That He will drive away from us all soul-corrupting passions and corrupting habits, and that He will implant in our hearts His divine fear, unto the fulfillment of His statutes, let us pray to the Lord.**

Filling some of our precious time by actively engaging in the battle for our souls would be a good use of the gift of time God has granted us.

* Sergius Bulgakov, *Churchly Joy: Orthodox Devotions for the New Year* (Grand Rapids, MI: Eerdmans Publishing Company, 2008), 43.
** From *The Great Book of Needs*, vol. IV (South Canaan, PA: St Tikhon's Seminary Press, 1999), 238.

The First Monday of January
Originally Written: January 2017

Redeeming the Time

Look carefully then how you walk, not as unwise men but as wise, making the most of the time, because the days are evil.
(Eph 5.15–16)

To "walk" – in the context of this epistle reading – is a metaphor for how we conduct our lives. We can live wisely or unwisely. Since wisdom as a gift from God is so essential to the biblical understanding of a human person drawing closer to the divine likeness, then to walk unwisely is to painfully undermine the integrity of our human nature, to live in a way that we become progressively *unlike* God. To put things another way, to walk unwisely would be to subject ourselves to the seeming whim of chance, rather than to the providence of a loving God. Walking with wisdom, on the other hand, depends on "making the most of the time." This can also be translated as "redeeming the time." To redeem the time is, first, not to waste it, especially on superfluous things or activities. More positively, it could mean to spend our time in worthwhile pursuits, seeking to do the good in all of life's various circumstances. We are children of God at all times, not only when we are in church or before the icons in our domestic prayer corner. How we live and how we interact with others is how we express our Christian faith on a daily basis.

The Apostle Paul notes, "The days are evil." In a fallen world, every single day presents us with the possibility – if not probability – of encountering evil on a limited or a grand scale. To believe that the days we are living in are somehow "not that bad" is wishful thinking, divorced from any rational perception of reality. We live at a time when people have forgotten God, and consequently we have lost sight of our basic humanity. For the forgetfulness of God can profoundly impact our understanding of the human person's role in the world in a decisively negative way. Any perception of our humanity that is disconnected from God as source and Creator results in the further perception that human beings are autonomous and alone in the world, subject to blind and impersonal forces. This kind of thinking essentially results in a debasement of humanity. Faith in God endows each person with integrity and a sense of both vocation and meaningful destiny.

To "redeem the time" involves *sanctifying* time, remembering and honoring the reality that the full expanse of our lives – our "lifetime" – is a gift from God. In the fallen world that we occupy, time has become inextricably linked to mortality and death, but it remains a gift, as do all aspects of God's creative will, now redeemed by the advent of Christ. Yet our Christian vocation is to "sanctify time," understanding temporality as our movement toward the kingdom which has no end. Every moment counts because every moment is a gift from God.

The civil New Year on January 1 evokes the unavoidable theme of time, prompting me to reread Archbishop Kallistos Ware's essay "Time: Prison or Path to Freedom?" The title alone hints at the deep ambivalence with which time imbues our human existence:

> How are we to regard time: an enemy or friend, as our prison or our path to freedom? Which aspect do we find predominant in its double-edged impact upon us: anguish or healing, terror or hope, decay or growth, separation or relationship?[*]

In other words, is time simply "eating away" at the successive and finite number of moments that comprise our lives, sweeping us

---

[*] "Time: Prison or Path to Freedom?" In Ware, *The Inner Kingdom* (Crestwood, NY: St Vladimir's Seminary Press, 2000), 181-192, here 183.

along toward death and oblivion, or is there purpose and a transcendent "destination" in this movement? This notion of transcendent destination helps us journey closer to the sanctification of time in our minds and hearts. As Ware suggests, time forces us to consider our response to these two poles of existence. Will we live with hope or despair? Will time be our prison or path to freedom? Will we walk unwisely or redemptively in time?

We can be "in the world" but not "of the world" if we choose to "make the most of the time, because the days are evil." How can we make the most of time? As I mentioned above, this boils down to encountering time as the path that leads us toward the kingdom. In practical terms, there are many ways we could recover this sense of time. For Ware, however, they all come back to love:

> Time is the setting that makes it possible for us to choose love. It is time that allows us to respond to God by our own free content, that enables our love to mature, that permits us to grow in love.*

To love freely, as Christ loved us, is to choose to make the most of time, to return to St Paul's admonishment. One of the key words here is *choose*. Is it really a hard choice? In my humble opinion, within the grace-filled life of the Church, the choices before us are very easy to make.

Here is a deceptively simple prayer (just try to put it into daily practice!) from the Optina Elders that teaches us how to redeem the time:

> O Lord, grant that I may meet all that this coming day brings to me with spiritual tranquility. Grant that I may fully surrender myself to Thy holy will.
>
> At every hour of this day, direct and support me in all things. Whatsoever news may reach me in the course of

---

* Ibid., 188-89.

the day, teach me to accept it with a calm soul and the firm conviction that all is subject to Thy holy will.

Direct my thoughts and feelings in all my words and actions. In all unexpected occurrences, do not let me forget that all is sent down from Thee.

Grant that I may deal straightforwardly with every member of my family, neither embarrassing nor saddening them.

O Lord, grant me to endure the fatigue of the coming day and all the events that will take place during it.

Direct my will and teach me to pray, to believe, to hope, to be patient, to forgive and to love.

Amen.[*]

Though it may sound rather simple, perhaps, as Orthodox Christians, we could redeem the time with the basic practices of daily prayer, the reading of the Scriptures, greater commitment to the liturgical life of the Church, prayerful preparation for the Eucharist, periodic confession of sins, and acts of kindness and compassion toward our neighbors. On closer consideration, these basics may be the actual "building blocks" that result in "being changed into his likeness from one degree of glory to another" (2 Cor 3.18). I am convinced that in such a way we would be moving toward redeeming the time.

---

[*] *Orthodox Daily Prayers* (South Canaan: St Tikhon Seminary Press, 1982).

The Second Monday of January
Originally Written: January 2015

Baptism: "When All Is Said and Done"

The aim of the Christian life is to return to that perfect grace of the most holy and life-giving Spirit, which was originally conferred upon us through divine baptism.
— St Ignatios Xanthopoulos and St Kallistos

Our recent celebration of the Feast of Theophany – the baptism of our Lord, God, and Savior Jesus Christ – provides a fitting context to reflect upon the great mystery of holy baptism. We can do this effectively by turning to the saints and theologians of the Church, who speak of the meaning of this sacrament. At times, what they say may seem "unrealistic," their rhetorical flourishes idealizing the more sober experience of baptism many of us encounter in real life. However, we should remember that the Fathers of the Church were "maximalists." To them, the life of Christ was something to live and share with others through their example and writings, however exuberantly. The Fathers always presented us with the fullness of the Gospel so that we, in turn, would not be tempted to reduce that same Gospel to the level of uninspiring moralism or conventional religious piety.

St Cyril of Alexandria († 444) explained how the Lord's baptism establishes the "pattern" for our own baptism. He linked baptism with unceasing prayer:

> It was necessary, therefore, that the Word of the Father, when He humbled Himself unto emptiness, and deigned to assume our likeness, should become for our sakes the pattern and way of every good work. For it follows, that He Who in everything is first, in this also set the example.

> In order, therefore, that we may learn both the power itself of holy baptism, and how much we gain by approaching so great a grace, He commences the work Himself; and having been baptized, prays that you, my beloved, may learn that never-ceasing prayer is a thing most fitting for those who have once been counted worthy of holy baptism. (*Commentary on Luke*, Homily 11)

Likewise, St Cyril of Jerusalem († 386) explained the meaning of a sacrament as a genuine participation in the reality of grace that lies hidden within – and conferred upon the participant – through the rite of the sacrament. In baptism, we imitate the death and resurrection of Christ, sacramentally dying and rising again with Christ in truth:

> O what a strange and inconceivable thing it is! We did not really die, we were not really buried; we were not crucified and raised again; our imitation of Christ was but in figure, while our salvation is truth. Christ actually was crucified and buried, and truly rose again; and all these things have been transmitted to us, that we might by imitation participate in his suffering, and so gain salvation in truth.*

A true baptism involves the invocation of the Holy Trinity, as Christ taught His disciples (Mt 28.16–20). This is an invocation that, as Fr George Florovsky points out, "is required because outside the Trinitarian faith it is impossible to know Christ, to recognize in Jesus the Incarnate Lord, 'One of the Holy Trinity.'"** Explaining the effect of the trinitarian invocation upon the person being baptized, St Nicholas Cabasilas in the fourteenth century wrote:

> It is the Father who is reconciled, the Son who reconciles, while the Holy Spirit is bestowed as a gift on those who have become friends.... It was needful, therefore, for those who call upon God over the divine washing to distinguish

---

* *The Mystagogical Catechesis*, II.5.
** *Creation and Redemption*, vol. III of *The Collected Works of Georges Florovsky* (Belmont, MA: Nordland Publishing Company, 1975), 149.

between the Persons by calling on the Father, the Son, and the Holy Spirit, as they provide the sacred re-creation which alone shows forth God as thus distinguished.*

The water of baptism destroys one life and reveals another; it drowns the old man and raises up the new. To be baptized is to be born according to Christ, to receive existence, to come into being out of nothing. And yet, a sacrament is not some form of magic, a mechanically bestowed grace that saves a person regardless of his level of commitment to Christ. The process of salvation – which we often refer to as *theosis* (deification) – is a synergistic process, a combination of divine grace and human freedom. The latter, human element implies a degree of struggle – we must cooperate with God if we are to experience the transforming grace of holy baptism. St Gregory of Nyssa († 395) said this well in his *Great Catechism*:

> If the life after initiation (baptism) is of the same quality as the uninitiated life (before baptism), then, though it may be a bold thing to say, I will say it without flinching; in the case of such people the water is merely water, for the gift of the Holy Spirit in no way shows itself in what takes place.... A child born to any one is entirely akin to his parent. If then you have received God, and have become a child of God, display in the purpose of your life the God that is in you, display in yourself the Father that gave you birth.

A great saint of the more recent past – Seraphim of Sarov († 1833) – places baptism in the context of one's whole earthly existence, a part of God's providential care for each of his "adopted" children. If life is indeed a period of testing, then the grace of baptism, which is nothing less than the gift of the Holy Spirit, gives us strength to prevail in this lifelong test of man on earth.

---

* *The Life in Christ*, trans. Carmino J. deCatanzaro (Crestwood, NY: St Vladimir's Seminary Press, 1974), 74.

> And what in the world can be higher and more precious than the gift of the Holy Spirit sent down to us from on high in the Sacrament of Baptism? This grace of Baptism is so great and indispensable, so vital for man, that it is not taken away even from a heretic until his death. That is, it is not taken away from him until the end of the period of appointment on high by God's providence as a lifelong test of man on earth – a test to see what a man can accomplish by means of the strength of grace given to him on high in the time allotted to him by God.*

Within the life of the Church, all theology is ultimately expressed through doxology – the living praise of the living God that brings joy and gladness to our spirits through the grace of the Holy Spirit. Doxology – the glorification of God – is a kind of prayerful or poeticized theology that allows us to approach the mystery of God in Christ with humility and praise. One of the many wonderful hymns of the Feast of Theophany summarizes its theological and spiritual content in a manner befitting the depth of its significance for us:

> The true Light has appeared, and grants enlightenment to all. Christ, Who is above all purity, is baptized with us; He sanctifies the water and it becomes a cleansing for our souls. The outward sign is earthly, the inward grace is higher than the heavens; Salvation comes through washing, and through water the Spirit: Descending into the water we ascend to God. Wonderful are Thy works, O Lord: Glory to Thee!**

And so, when all is said and done, we approach God and sing "glory to Thee!"

---

* Constantine Cavarnos and Mary-Barbara Zeldin, *St Seraphim of Sarov*, vol. 5 of *Modern Orthodox Saints* (Belmont, MA: Institute for Byzantine and Modern Greek Studies, 1980), 107.
** Mother Mary and Archimandrite Kallistos Ware, *The Festal Menaion*, 382-383.

The Third Monday of January
Originally Written: January 2003

Rebuking the Tempter and Following Jesus

Earlier this week, we celebrated the Leavetaking of Theophany. A "theophany" is an open manifestation of God, and the Feast of Theophany commemorates the revelation of the Holy Trinity at the Jordan River. As St John Chrysostom says: "Why, then, is this day called Theophany? Because Christ made himself known to all – not then when He was born – but then when He was baptized. Until this time He was not known to the people." It was His baptism at the hands of the Forerunner that inaugurated the public ministry of Christ that began with words recorded in the Gospels and continues to call through the centuries to this day to shake humanity out of a false sense of complacency: "Repent, for the Kingdom of Heaven is at hand" (Mt 4.17). According to Christ, there is something more to life than ordinary joys and sorrows. Acknowledging this with thanksgiving, the very pinnacle of our communal worship of God in the Liturgy begins by "blessing" the kingdom of the Father, Son, and Holy Spirit.

Yet before the Lord began demonstrating the kingdom of heaven's presence through His words and deeds, an additional significant event prepared Him for His messianic ministry: the temptation in the wilderness (Mt 4.1–11; Mk 1.12–13; Lk 4.1–13). The nuances of the Greek term used to describe this event (*peirasmos*) allows us to think in terms of a "temptation" or "testing." In a sense, Christ was tested when God allowed Him to be tempted by the devil. In the process, Christ rejected an image of the Messiah that would project a worldly or political show of force. Contrary to popular expectations, as the Messiah of Israel, Christ would be the Suffering

Servant who defeated the devil on the cross through self-sacrificial love rather than defeating the hated Romans by militant means. In this the Lord was obedient to the will of the Father, an obedience freely chosen in and through the human will that was assumed in the incarnation. It is this same obedience that will lead Christ to His salvific death on the cross.

It is highly significant that it was the Holy Spirit who "led" Jesus "into the wilderness to be tempted by the devil" (Mt 4.1). Nothing in the life of Christ is accidental. He is thus led into this barren landscape by His heavenly Father who acts through the Holy Spirit, and this "face-to-face" encounter with the evil one is no exception. The austere and unsettling figure of Dostoevsky's Grand Inquisitor refers to the devil as "the dread and intelligent spirit, the spirit of self-destruction and non-being" (*The Brothers Karamazov*). This dread spirit tempted Christ through the three questions, each of which tested His fidelity to His unique messianic vocation as willed by His heavenly Father. Dostoevsky, through the tragic figure of the Grand Inquisitor, further reveals the power and non-human source of these powerful temptations:

> By the questions alone, simply by the miracle of their appearance, one can see that one is dealing with a mind not human and transient but eternal and absolute. For in these three questions all of subsequent human history is as if brought together into a single whole and foretold; three images are revealed that will take in all the insoluble historical contradictions of human nature over all the earth.

In other words, these three temptations were not "invented" or "made up" by the evangelists for dramatic effect. The very "perfection" of the temptations posed by the devil reveal their veracity.

And what are these three temptations? According to St Matthew's account, as Jesus was fasting, the devil posed these three temptations to Him: for Jesus to change stones into bread; to reveal His divine identity by throwing himself down from the pinnacle of the temple so that God can save Him; and to worship the devil in exchange for the "kingdoms of the world" (cf. Mt 4.1–11). In Dostoevsky's profound interpretation of Christ's encounter with the tempter in the wilderness, Jesus refuses to receive obedience through miracle, mystery, and authority as represented in these three tantalizing temptations. By compelling human beings to believe in Him by overwhelming them with the miraculous; by exploiting a sense of mystery to attract human beings to follow Him; and by appealing to the human need for security through external authority, Christ would have accepted and approved of a distorted understanding of human nature. In Dostoevsky's understanding of Christ, as attainable as these "powers" may be for the Son of God, each one in its own way violates the gift of human freedom given to us by God and appealed to by Christ. It is for this very reason that Christ did not come down from the cross, as He was "tempted" to do by those who mocked Him. Even if freedom is a burden as well as a gift, it is the true vision of humanity created "in the image and likeness of God." We, in turn, freely choose to follow Christ, the crucified "Lord of glory."

Dostoevsky had specific concerns when he used the temptation in the wilderness to dramatize the dialectics of human freedom and coercion in *The Brothers Karamazov*. Within the context of the Gospels, we can say that Christ had to overcome the temptation to be a messiah who was not in accord with the will of God. He was not declared to be His Father's "beloved Son" at the Jordan River to be a militant messiah who ruled through power. The words of God the Father at the Jordan were clear echoes from the Suffering Servant songs of the prophet Isaiah, a servant who would heal us by His stripes – His very suffering would be redemptive. Therefore, the suffering on the cross was essential to the divine economy. To overcome such temptations as man, the Lord resorted to prayer and fasting in the wilderness – the spiritual weapons given to us all in the Church for precisely the same purpose in the "wilderness" of a fallen world: to strengthen the inner person against false and pretentious promises. We can accomplish this by relying on "every word that proceeds from the mouth of God" (Deut 8.3). We further heed the words, "You shall not tempt the Lord your God" (Deut 6.16). And we also follow Christ who reminded us: "You shall worship the Lord your God and him only shall you serve" (Deut 6.13). Christ refuted the evil one's false counsel by the power of these scriptural words. Another clear lesson for us in our relationship with the Holy Scriptures. As the dawn of a new humanity, Jesus re-enacted the history of Israel, but he "passes" the type of test that Israel "failed" to pass in its earlier forty-year wanderings in the wilderness. In fact, as the new and last Adam, He reversed the effects of Adam's disobedience through His faithful obedience to the Father. It may sound startling to us today, but Jesus was "perfected" precisely through obedience (cf. Heb 5.8).

Our human will was healed by the human will the Son of God assumed and united to His divine will in the incarnation. Before the garden of Gethsemane, the perfect expression of that healing through obedience may just be the temptation/testing in the wilderness. In a way that may seem distressingly paradoxical to us today, it is precisely meaningful obedience in the spiritual life that strengthens our human nature on a very personal basis. As such, obedience to God further strengthens our freedom in our ongoing battle with temptation. As the final temptation was beaten back by Christ, He could say to the tempter: "Be gone, Satan!" Our goal is to be able to rebuke the tempter with the same words when we are also tempted and tested – however often that may be.

The Fourth Monday of January
Originally Written: March 2017

A "Pouring Out of Long Accumulating, Long Pent-up Pain"

For some time now, Presvytera Deborah and I have been reading Elizabeth Gaskell's classic biography *The Life of Charlotte Brontë* together.* Originally published in 1857, this book has been praised as the greatest biography of nineteenth-century English literature. Charlotte Brontë († 1855) is the creator of Jane Eyre, one of British literature's most memorable characters. All readers of this novel know that "plain Jane" is a high-spirited and perceptive young woman who possesses a rich inner life that has endeared her to countless readers since the novel's initial publication in 1847. Countless stage and film adaptations of Jane's story continue to be produced to this day. Yet Brontë also wrote other fine novels, including *The Professor, Villette,* and *Shirley.*

Charlotte Brontë had a deep Christian faith and sensibility. Her faith was severely tested as she first nursed, and then helplessly watched, three of her siblings die within about a six-month period (September 1848-May 1849). Two of these siblings were also novelists: Emily wrote the famous *Wuthering Heights* and Anne wrote *The Tenant of Wildfell Hall.* Emily was twenty-nine when she died, Anne was twenty-seven. The third and oldest sibling that Charlotte lost in this period was her deeply troubled brother, Branwell, who was thirty-one years old at the time of his death. This was a series of crushing losses for Charlotte. Her deeply personal and poignant letters written in the aftermath of these untimely deaths testify to her belief in eternal life with God through Jesus Christ, our "Redeemer," as she often referred to Christ.

* (New York: Penguin Classics, 1997).

Her father, Patrick Brontë, was a curate of the local Anglican parish in Haworth, and their home in the parsonage there is now a place of pilgrimage for Brontë devotees. Charlotte Brontë was fiercely Protestant, and just as fiercely hostile to Roman Catholicism. Supposedly, she both pitied and feared Roman Catholics.

When she taught at the Pensionnat Heger, a school for girls in predominantly Catholic Brussels, Belgium, she felt surrounded by "Romanism." She further thought that her Roman Catholic students were filled with superstition and were susceptible to "sensual indulgence." Yet, before we judge Charlotte Brontë too harshly for such prejudices, such antagonism between Protestants and Roman Catholics in nineteenth-century England was probably typical for that milieu. Every time and place seemingly has its own prejudices – we certainly have ours.

All of which makes one peculiar event in her life all the more remarkable and difficult to fully explain. Wandering through Brussels during a break from teaching, and at a time when she was suffering from a certain malaise that we would term despondency, if not depression, she found herself entering the large Roman Catholic Cathedral of St Michael and St Gudula for what seems to have been the evening service, what we would call Vespers. Following the service, she made her way to that part of the cathedral where the ornate confessional boxes were located. And at this point, something compelled her to enter one of the confessionals and confess to a Roman Catholic priest.

As one prominent Brontë scholar – Helen Cooper – has written: "A daughter of a Church of England clergyman, Brontë must have been desperately depressed to have decided that her only hope of comfort lay in thus violating Protestant-Catholic 'rules.'" It took her some effort to convince the priest to even hear her confession as she informed him that she was a Protestant. Charlotte later wrote of this incident: "I was determined to confess," and after the priest relented to hear her – presumably because it might lead to her conversion – she emphatically added: "I actually did confess – a real confession."

To this day, there is no memoir or letter that reveals precisely what she confessed on that day in Brussels. However, in the words of her most autobiographical character – the ultra-Protestant Lucy Snowe from the novel *Villette* after *she* confessed under the exact same conditions – we read the following:

> [T]he mere relief of communication in an ear which was human and sentient, yet consecrated – the mere pouring out of some portion of long accumulating, long pent-up pain into a vessel whence it could not be again diffused – had done me good. I was already solaced.

Charlotte Brontë never went to confession again, but nevertheless acknowledged in these words of the fictional Lucy Snowe a truly deep experience. Perhaps this was a once-in-a-lifetime concession to that inner need to "confess your sins to one another" (Jas 5.16), a longing I am sure we all have within us.

As we approach Great Lent, a season when our own confession becomes a key component of our spiritual effort as Orthodox Christians, I am reflecting on this real and literary event from the life and literature of Charlotte Brontë. (I wonder, by the way, what the ultra-Protestant Charlotte Brontë would have thought of our Byzantine Liturgy.) We, of course, may feel that confession is merely an "obligation" to fulfill as a member of the Church. I even ask my parishioners to schedule their confessions by appointment, which lacks the spontaneity of confessing out of some urgent, inner need akin to that of Charlotte.

However, we too may be surprised by what we experience in confession. We (perhaps desperately) need to "unburden our souls" to resort to something of a meaningful cliché. Every confession has the potential to help us "break on through to the other side," to quote a song by the Doors. Such a breakthrough is the path to inner freedom. The sacrament of confession offers the supreme opportunity to overcome a bad habit, a disposition, a passion; to seek forgiveness of our sins against God and one another; or to remove those obstacles that we perversely create between ourselves and the living God. And, as Orthodox Christians, we have the liberty of not having to overcome any prejudices concerning confession. We need only overcome any reluctance or resistance; any self-justification or self-defense; or any illusions about ourselves that we refuse to abandon, so that we also may experience "the mere pouring out of some portion of long accumulating, long pent-up pain" to a priest "consecrated" for that very role.

As different as we are from Charlotte Brontë – though the "human condition" remains the same – there is no reason we could not fully agree with her when she said that confession "had done [her] good."

The Fifth Monday of January
Originally Written: February 2014

Ascending with Zacchaeus

Today salvation has come to this house. (Lk 19.9)

On the first pre-lenten Sunday of the liturgical year, we have the first signal that the Great Fast is approaching. This sign is Zacchaeus Sunday, which occurs five Sundays and four weeks prior to the start of Great Lent. (With these five special Sundays, no one can claim that Great Lent caught him/her unaware. The Church gives us ample "warning" for the seismic shift that Great Lent will bring to our lifestyles.) Zacchaeus Sunday is based upon the gospel account of how Zacchaeus and his household were saved by the healing and forgiving presence of Christ (Lk 19.1–10). This was in response to Zacchaeus' conversion and his repentance before the Lord. It is interesting that we have the name of this publican – perhaps he was a known member of the earliest post-resurrection Christian community centered in Jerusalem yet scattered throughout Israel. Whatever the case, this conversion had a strong impact on the early Church, as this account was recorded by the evangelist Luke.

In a relatively short, yet very dramatic narrative, St Luke vividly brings to life not only the encounter between Zacchaeus and Christ, but a series of profoundly interconnected themes that deserve our close attention:

- desire
- repentance
- atonement
- salvation

Zacchaeus, as Fr Alexander Schmemann wrote in his now classic study *Great Lent*, is a man of "desire."* It was his burning desire "to see who Jesus was" (Lk 19.3) that led him to "climb up into a sycamore tree to see him" (19.4). Though Zacchaeus was despised as a publican, or tax collector, that same position gave him a certain begrudged "prominence." Thus, the spectacle of Zacchaeus scrambling up the sycamore tree likely exposed him to public ridicule. This desire to "see Jesus" can lead anyone to overcome many of his or her human limitations, as well as the fear of violating any of the accepted rules of social etiquette if necessary. Our human frailty, that sinfulness that leaves us all short of the glory of God (Rom 3.23), is represented here by Zacchaeus being "small of stature" (Lk 19.3). Our own sinfulness cuts us down to size and leaves us short of the stature of Christ that we are meant to grow into. A desire to change is the first movement onto the path of this desired growth. In hearing or reading this passage, we learn to humble ourselves in the knowledge that the sinful publican Zacchaeus has attained a stature we are to emulate, "the measure of the stature of the fullness of Christ" (Eph 4.13).

Once Zacchaeus and his household are blessed with the presence of Christ, he openly repents of having "defrauded anyone of anything" (Lk 19.8). His heart has been wounded by the love of Christ who, in turn, suffered the reproach and murmuring of the witnesses of this event for being "the guest of a man who is a sinner" (19.7). Zacchaeus atones for his former sinfulness by openly declaring "Behold, Lord, the half of my goods I give to the poor; and if I have defrauded anyone of anything, I restore it fourfold" (19.8). This is not a legalistic transaction. Zacchaeus is not purchasing the favor of God. Rather, he is moved to a concrete expression of a changed life that goes far beyond mere words or internal disposition.

* (Crestwood, NY: St Vladimir's Seminary Press, 1969), 17-18.

The unmerited gift of salvation is how Christ "seals" the initial movement of Zacchaeus toward the restoration of his full stature. Salvation (*soteria*) means wholeness, the wholeness of soul and body that only God can restore. Zacchaeus has received this gift of salvation because "he also is a son of Abraham" (19.9). This proclamation ran contrary to certain elements then popular within Jewish piety that would have marginalized him as a religious and social pariah. The salvation of Christ is extensive and intensive: universally offered to all people, and to the worst of sinners. This is crystallized by Christ's solemn pronouncement that closes the narrative concerning Zacchaeus: "For the Son of man came to seek and save the lost" (19.10). All – Jew and Gentile, the righteous and the unrighteous – are lost, but God "desires all men to be saved and to come to the knowledge of the truth" (1 Tim 2.4).

In one of the many fine paradoxes or ironies found in the Gospels, the despised publican Zacchaeus becomes our teacher: "So the last shall be first, and the first last" (Mt 20.16). When that sinks in deeply, we can begin our own ascent to God on the ladder of the virtues as Zacchaeus ascended his humble sycamore tree.

The First Monday of February
Originally Written: February 2016

If St John Chrysostom Had Watched the Super Bowl

The Super Bowl – and with it the so-called Super Sunday – is now over. This colossal social phenomenon is viewed by hundreds of millions of people every year. In North America, at least, the Super Bowl has become something of a secular "pascha." There is a "pre-feast" of preparation, hype, and pre-game analysis; and there is a "post-feast" of further analysis and restoration to life's usual rhythms. Following this last game, I have found myself wondering how someone like St John Chrysostom, who fell asleep in the Lord in AD 407, would have approached the Super Bowl phenomenon in his own unique and pastoral manner. Of course, there is a huge chronological gap between St John's time and our own, but we also know that there "is nothing new under the sun" (Eccl 1.9) and we can discover some very close parallels just under the surface when comparing different eras and their cultures. St John well knew and understood the lure of the "games" and other forms of public entertainment in his own time, as he lived in cosmopolitan urban centers such as Constantinople and Antioch. Such cities invariably had a hippodrome – like today's stadiums – at the center of a teeming social milieu that was hungry for public entertainment.

In St John's pastoral approach, criticism was never his main objective, even when there was implicit ridicule of public entertainment (for example, when he criticized the "theater" as it existed in his day). He would reference athletic events and other forms of entertainment to exhort his flock to be vigilant and committed in its adherence to and practice of the Gospel. Being a "fan" of a sport is far from being a "member" of the Church. As a pastor, St

John challenged his flock to ensure that the great gap in that distinction was not somehow closed by lack of vigilance.

The great saint was fully aware of a kind of nominal membership in the Church, and he was quick to point out how erosive of genuine faith that lack of commitment could be for the entire flock under his pastoral care. St John was basically asking whether Christians were as committed to the Gospel and the life of the Church as they were adherents, participants, and performers in the "entertainment industry" of the fourth and fifth centuries. Primarily, this would include athletes and actors. Do Christians show the same level of passion for the Gospel as do the fans of the games and theater? Here is one example among many of how St John used his rhetorical skills – replete with both sarcasm and humor – to challenge Christians on this front:

> We run eagerly to dances and amusements. We listen with pleasure to the foolishness of singers. We enjoy the foul words of actors for hours without getting bored. And yet when God speaks we yawn, we scratch ourselves and feel dizzy. Most peoples would run rabidly to the horse track, although there is no roof there to protect the audience from rain, even when it rains heavily or when the wind is lifting everything. They don't mind bad weather or the cold or the distance. Nothing keeps them in their homes. When they are about to go to church, however, then the soft rain becomes an obstacle to them. And if you ask them who Amos or Obadiah is, or how many prophets or apostles there are, they can't even open their mouths. Yet they can tell you every detail about the horses, the singers and the actors. What kind of state is this?

This rhetorical deflation of the theater and games serves as a backdrop that only intensifies the strength of his descriptions of the manifold riches of the Church, especially the Eucharist. From the same homily, here is St John's impassioned and rhetorically brilliant description of the glory of the Church:

> The Church is the foundation of virtue and the school of spiritual life. Just cross its threshold at any time, and immediately you forget daily cares. Pass inside, and a spiritual ray will surround your soul. This stillness causes awe and teaches the Christian life. It raises up your train of thought and doesn't allow you to remember present things. It transports you from earth to Heaven. And if the gain is so great when a worship service is not even taking place, just think, when the Liturgy is performed – and the prophets teach, the Apostles preach the Gospel, Christ is among believers, God the Father accepts the performed sacrifice, and the Holy Spirit grants His own rejoicing – what great benefit floods those who have attended church as they leave the church. The joy of anyone who rejoices is preserved in the Church. The gladness of the embittered, the rejoicing of the saddened, the refreshment of the tortured, the comfort of the tired, all are found in the Church. Because Christ says, 'Come to me, all who are tired and heavy-laden, and I will give you rest' [Mt 11.28]. What is more longed for than [to hear] this Voice? What sweeter than this invitation? The Lord is calling you to a Banquet when He invites you to church. He urges you to be comforted from toils and He transports you to a place of comfort from pain, because He lightens you from the burden of sins. He heals distress with spiritual enjoyment, and sadness with joy.

St John was not called "Chrysostom" – the "Golden-mouthed" – for nothing! He does not admonish his flock in this homily to give up on the games and other forms of entertainment; but he surely makes it clear that there is no comparison between the two. And that, therefore, our desire and commitment cannot be so misplaced to somehow put the two on the same level of attraction. The perfectly legitimate desire to "fit in" with one's neighbors and participate in socially popular events must be balanced by an awareness of not being fully of the world once one is baptized into the Church.

Bearing all of that in mind, if I were to write in the spirit of St John regarding parish life in the contemporary world, I would make the following pastoral recommendations based on the recent Super Bowl (or for that matter, any existing commitment we might have to the world of professional sports/entertainment):

- If you watched the Super Bowl from its opening kick-off to the end of the game, but if you chronically arrive late for the opening doxology of "Blessed is the Kingdom" at the Liturgy, then it may be time to show the same commitment to the Liturgy and arrive at the beginning. That opening doxological statement opens us up to a reality hardly matched by an opening kick-off.

- If you spent time watching all the pre-game hype and analysis, but you don't arrive before the Liturgy for the reading of the hours or Matins (depending on the custom of your jurisdiction), then I would suggest coming to church before the actual Liturgy begins – a mere 20 minutes. This way you can settle in and calm down a bit in preparation for the Liturgy that will shortly unfold in all its majesty.

- If you have been engaged in some of the (endless) post-game analysis since last Sunday, or watched "highlights" of the game, or recall some of the more significant and game-changing plays of the game, but you struggle by mid-week to remember what the Gospel was at last Sunday's Liturgy, then I would suggest engaging in some post-Liturgy analysis of the Gospel you heard on any given Sunday. Would it be too much to return to that Sunday's Gospel for another post-Liturgy reading that may yield further insights after hearing it in church together with the homily? Such "analysis" can eventually become genuine meditation of even contemplation.

All of this is more than possible, according to St John, because of the inexhaustible riches of the Liturgy. Once again, he exhorts us to leave the Liturgy as changed human beings, having communed of the risen Lord:

> Let us depart from the Divine Liturgy like lions who are producing fire, having become fearsome even to the devil, because the holy Blood of the Lord that we commune waters our souls and gives us great strength. When we commune of it worthily, it chases the demons far away and brings the angels and the Lord of the angels near us. This Blood is the salvation of our souls; with this the soul is washed, with this it is adorned. This Blood makes our minds brighter than fire; this makes our souls brighter than gold.

We are slowly drawing near to the Church's own "Super Sunday" which is, of course, Pascha. Let our preparation and desire for that day surpass any of our other passions or commitments, for the Lord taught us, "Where your treasure is, there will your heart be also" (Mt 6.21).

The Second Monday of February
Originally Written: February 2009

An Infant's Burial

Yesterday, we served *The Order for the Burial of an Infant* on behalf of a two-day old boy who died at Children's Hospital on Saturday.

Humanly speaking, there is nothing more heartbreaking than this: a tiny infant dressed in white baptismal clothes, lying in the middle of the church in a coffin that looks more like a small box, surrounded by his grieving family and friends. With an open casket, I was deeply struck by the innocence, purity, and beauty of this "undefiled infant," as he was called in the funeral service. It was difficult *not* to keep returning to his coffin and looking at him. It was a moving image that will always remain with me. In addition, we witnessed his poor mother, still recovering from giving birth on Friday, together with a father who was momentarily elated with the birth of his firstborn son, joined together in mutual grief at their little son's burial service. The initial impact of death is that of irrevocable loss; the lament from the funeral service is our own: "I weep and wail when I think upon death."

A completely different funeral service is used for infants, which in the Church includes basically all children under the age of seven. In my years as a priest, this was the first time I had ever served this particular funeral office. I was struck by the beauty of the service, the certainty of an infant's entrance into the kingdom of God, and the complete absence of prayers for the "forgiveness of sins" of the departed infant – there is no sin for which he needs to be forgiven, including so-called "original sin." The service explicitly states that "he has not transgressed Thy divine command" (Ode

6 of the Canon); and that "infants have done no evil" (Ode 9 of the Canon). Since transgressing the divine commandment is inevitable in a fallen world, we pray over a departed adult that God will forgive his or her sins. But for an infant, the service repeatedly refers to the departed infant as "undefiled," "uncorrupted," "most-pure," "truly blessed," and even "holy."

This is not sentimentalism meant to make us feel better, it reveals a profound theological truth. A child, according to Orthodox Christian teaching, is not born a "guilty sinner." He or she is not baptized in order to wash away the stain of "original sin" with its attendant guilt. We believe that a child is born bearing the *consequences* of "original sin," often referred to as "ancestral sin" by Orthodox theologians precisely to distinguish it from "original sin." The consequences of ancestral sin are corruption and death. A child is born into a fallen, broken, and corrupted world, grievously wounded by sin and death. There is nothing sentimental in that assessment of our human condition! Disease and physical deformities are a part of this world – caused by humankind's initial alienation from God – and providentially allowed by God. Therefore, a child is never too young to die. The nature of life is tragic, and nowhere is this more clearly revealed than in the death of an innocent young child. An infant is baptized in order to be saved from the consequences of the ancestral sin that led every person inevitably to sin and be subject to corruption and death. The child needs to be "born again of water and the Spirit" – the mystery of baptism – to "put on Christ" and the gift of immortality that is received only through sacramentally partaking of the death and resurrection of Christ.

The entire funeral service was permeated by the sure hope and conviction that this little child has been "translated unto Thee," and that he is now "a partaker of Thy Heavenly good things" (Ode 6 of the Canon). His death is treated realistically, and the pathos of an uncompleted earthly life is clearly acknowledged. Yet his death is also his entrance into life with God in His eternal kingdom:

> By Thy righteous judgment, Thou hast cut down like a green herb before it has completely sprouted, the infant that Thou hast taken, O Lord. But, as Thou hast led him unto the divine mountain of eternal good things, do Thou plant him there, O Word. (Ode 5 of the Canon)

> The sword of death has come and cut thee off like a young branch, O blessed one that has not been tempted by worldly sweetness. But, lo, Christ openeth the heavenly gates unto thee, joining thee unto the elect, since He is deeply compassionate. (Ode 5 of the Canon)

> O Most-perfect Word, Who didst reveal Thyself as perfect Infant: Thou hast taken unto Thyself an infant imperfect in growth. Give him rest with all the Righteous who have been well-pleasing unto Thee, O only Lover of mankind. (Ode 3 of the Canon)

The suffering hearts of the mother and father are not forgotten in the prayers of the service, expressed with a certain rhetorical style that may no longer be fashionable, but which retains a genuinely poignant realism:

> No one is more pitiful than a mother, and no one is more wretched than a father, for their inward beings are troubled when they send forth their infants before them. Great is the pain of their hearts because of their children. (*Ikos* following Ode 6 of the Canon)

This is further intensified in a hymn that seeks to articulate the words of the infant as if he could communicate with those left behind. Here we find a realistic acknowledgement of intense grief, suffused with a certain hope that God can bring relief to that very grief:

> O God, God, Who hast summoned me: Be Thou the consolation of my household now, for a great lamentation has befallen them. For all have fixed their gaze on me, having

me as their only-begotten one. But do Thou, Who wast born of a Virgin Mother, refresh the inward parts of my mother, and bedew the heart of my father with this: Alleluia. (*Ikos* following Ode 6 of the Canon)

These hymns and prayers are profoundly comforting, not primarily for psychological and emotional reasons, but because they reveal what is essentially *true*: that Christ has overcome death, trampling it down on our behalf by His glorious resurrection. Death itself has been transformed from within. Horror and darkness give way to hope and life. The healing grace of God does not come through pious, psychological or emotional sentiment, but through the awareness of this truth as it penetrates our minds and hearts through the gift of faith. What other kind of "comfort" can there be when parents, relatives and friends must bear the cross of the death of a beloved infant? Grief and sorrow over such a loss never leave us, but they can be transmuted and transformed in time by the joy of knowing God's love, poured out to us through His beloved Son and our Savior, Jesus Christ.

The Third Monday of February
Originally Written: May 2011

The Heresy of the Rapture

Recently, a small group of fundamentalist Christians who are awaiting the "rapture" has been in the news. Yesterday, I happened to read an article about the self-appointed "preacher" of this group who found himself "flabbergasted" that the rapture did not actually materialize on the date he predicted (May 21, 2011). It seems he has gone into hiding (though not before announcing a revised date for the rapture, which is to be some time in October). His poor followers have been left to pick up the pieces of their shattered dream and return to the endless daily crosses we often must bear in the quotidian reality of this world.

For those who are blissfully ignorant of rapture theology, a short description may be helpful. Proponents of the rapture claim that Jesus will descend from heaven and "take up" true believing Christians into the air with Him – hence the term "rapture," from the Latin *raptio*, "to snatch." (The result of such an event would, naturally, be chaos. Hence the fictional representations of the post-rapture that depict planes crashing and cars careening around the streets and freeways, their drivers having been taken up.) Christ will then essentially return to heaven with the true believers He has raptured. They will be spared the seven years of tribulation unleashed upon the earth before Christ returns to inaugurate the end of the world and the last judgment. Thus, rapture beliefs advocate a two-part second coming of Christ that has no biblical or creedal support. This scenario offers the false comfort to Christians that they will not have to share the sufferings of the world with their fellow human beings, legitimately prophesied in the Scriptures, a blatant contradiction to the Scriptures (see Mt 24.21–22).

A belief in the rapture has never been part of the Church's Tradition but is rather credited to a certain John Darby († 1882). This "theology" is painfully superficial and artificial, based upon a misreading of a few biblical texts (c.f. 1 Thess 4.13–18; Mt 24.39–42; Jn 14.1–2). More recently, the *Left Behind* novel series popularized "rapture theology" with somewhat disastrous results; many Christians were taken in by this bogus and fear-creating depiction of the eschatological future. Admittedly, one can understand the attraction of apocalyptic literature, especially in a post-9/11 world. Many Christians feel disoriented in a rapidly secularizing culture that is simultaneously experiencing the anger of fundamentalist Islam. Perhaps some find comfort from their anxieties in an apocalyptic scenario that allows for ultimate vindication and security within God's eternal plan. An important irony, however, is that many biblical literalists cannot support their claims from the Scriptures – the word "rapture," for example, does not appear in the Bible! It is an artificial construction, based on cutting and pasting together the biblical passages mentioned above. There is also a strong militarist "right-wing" component to the *Left Behind* series that has political implications for American foreign policy concerning the state of Israel. Fortunately, it does seem as though a good deal of this has died down in recent years as this series of books has lost some of its momentum. Admittedly, I've never had the slightest temptation to read any of this literature, not even for the sake of maintaining an awareness of what was attracting so much attention.

As Orthodox Christians, we believe in the second coming (or *Parousia*) of Christ. The Nicene Creed proclaims: "He will come again with glory to judge the living and the dead." But Orthodox theologians do not waste time trying to calculate the time of the Parousia, nor do they attempt to describe what is essentially indescribable. Vigilance and preparedness are essential virtues according to the teaching of Christ. Our own deaths will come soon enough, and these will serve as our "personal judgments" before the final judgment for which we pray to have a "good defense."

There is more than enough there to occupy us in the interval. As a Serbian proverb says: "Work as if you will live to be a hundred, pray as if you will die tomorrow." One of the drearier effects of these stories is that it gives the media and non-believers leverage to mock Christians or Christianity for their zeal over what has turned out to be an un-fulfilled prophecy. There are entire websites devoted to ridiculing this latest group and their vigilance in waiting to be raptured on May 21 – there were even "rapture parties." The gleeful chatter and cynicism of the unbelieving world was very much a part of this sad story. Christianity remains, in some minds, a religion preoccupied with "judgment day" and the fear of God, together with God's wrath toward sin and disbelief. Perhaps this criticism is well-deserved in some cases, but it keeps the Gospel on the defensive and sends confusing signals as to what various Christians believe. Focus is taken off the love of God expressed so powerfully in the incarnation, death, and resurrection of Christ; of the sacramental life of the Church; of a life of serious prayer; and of the joy in the hearts of believers who trust in the further fulfillment of the promises of God.

Finally, there are the deeply disappointed, disenchanted, confused, and bewildered Christians who believed this "prophet." Many of them distributed their assets and could be facing a bleak future of readjustment to life in the world. What do they do now? Who will they listen to now? How many will abandon their faith in Christ as they will feel as if Christ "let them down"? I sympathize with these people and hope that they can put their lives back together again on a solid footing and with their basic Christian faith intact, though with a greater capacity for true discernment and a better knowledge of the Scriptures.

Just a few thoughts on yet another failed prophecy on the end of the world. Apparently, it's back to work for everyone.

The Fourth Monday of February
Originally Written: February 2017

Now Is the Acceptable Time: Lent as Beginning

A "good beginning" to Great Lent can go a long way toward a "good ending." Today is often referred to in the Church as Clean Monday, the first day of Great Lent. It may seem premature – if not a bit ludicrous – to already allude to the end of Great Lent so soon. We are just beginning our lenten journey, and the end is nowhere in sight, but I bring this up with a pastoral purpose in mind. In previous years, I have raised the question, "Is there life after Lent?" With this question in mind, I am asking how we can take some of the good and wholesome practices from Great Lent with us once the season is over. How often do we immediately go back to our earlier patterns of living as if Great Lent never really occurred, as though Lent were a pious interlude interrupting the "normal" way of living we eagerly return to after the ordeal is over? After Great Lent, the fasting element of the season may come to an end, but there is hopefully more to the season than adherence to fasting rules.

Bearing this type of approach and experience in mind, I would offer the following pastoral and practical advice: is there some practice, habit or attitude in your life *right now* that you very much desire to eliminate from your life? Or, to pose that question with a bit more bluntness, is there any such thing in your life that you *should* eliminate from your life as a Christian? Something sinful or at least something that undermines your relationship with God and your neighbor? With some effort, determination and focus – nourished by prayer, humility and a reliance on the grace of God – why not let this Lent be the "beginning of the end" of that practice, habit, or attitude that you desire to overcome once and for all? Then there would indeed be "life after Lent!" Taking Lent seriously forces us to come to terms with our sinful inclinations, and serves as the appointed opportunity to face up to and struggle against those very inclinations with their eradication as our goal.

If we look to our profound spiritual tradition, we know how the great saints of the past cataloged the more universal and characteristic "bad habits" that afflict us to one degree or another. The Fathers called these bad habits or vices "passions" (*pathi*) and believed they undermined a "purity of heart." The classic list of the eight passions, first drawn up by Evagrius of Pontus († 399) – often called the "psychologist of the desert" – included gluttony, lust, avarice, anger, dejection, spiritual despondency (or *acedia*), vanity, and pride.

A certain self-love – here understood as an unhealthy self-absorption or self-regard – is the "mother of the passions" according to Evagrius. We hear about these passions and their harmful spiritual effect in the *Great Canon of Repentance* celebrated during this first week of the Fast:

> A soiled garment clothes me – one shamefully stained with blood flowing from a life of passion and love of fleshly things.
>
> I fell beneath the weight of the passions and the corruption of my flesh, and from that moment has the Enemy had power over me.
>
> Instead of seeking poverty of spirit, I prefer a life of greed and self-gratification; therefore, O Savior, a heavy weight hangs from my neck.

Rhetoric or reality? You have to decide for yourself as you stand quietly in church as these verses from the Great Canon ring out.

Actually, these passions begin as "thoughts" (*logismoi*) that assail the mind. (Hence, the catalog of sins above may occasionally be referred to as the "eight thoughts.") When entertained and acted upon, the thought enters and lodges itself in the heart. Once rooted there, it is difficult to uproot that particular passion. What may begin as a temptation from the evil one will eventually become an ingrained action or attitude that has gained control over us. We are then basically "programmed" to return to that thought or action as our will to resist has become thoroughly weakened. Thus, what is an "unnatural" passion — because it is sinful — becomes quite "natural" to us after endless repetition. In contemporary vocabulary, perhaps we could even think of these passions as addictions, although that term is usually reserved for substance abuse. Yet, according to our spiritual tradition, we can become as "addicted" to gluttony, avarice, or pride as others may be to alcohol or drugs. The goal is not merely to eliminate the passions, but to replace them with virtues. Can gluttony and lust be replaced by self-control? Avarice by generosity? Anger by patience or even meekness? Vanity and pride by humility? The spiritual life is not just a negative battle (warfare *against* the passions), it is the positive effort to acquire virtues.

Is there anything in that list that we need to work on overcoming? The very universality of the list makes that a real possibility. Is anyone just sick and tired of doing the same thing over and over, even when we know it is detrimental to our lives or relationships? Only by acknowledging this destruction can we seriously enter into battle against a certain passion.

Perhaps that all sounds a bit "heavy." Yet there are many other simple yet positive actions to embrace as we begin Great Lent. Acts of kindness, concern, and compassion, perhaps. Do we need to visit a sick friend or call a housebound aunt on the phone more often than we are now doing? Do we need to work at becoming a more positive presence in our work environment? Can we work at becoming more considerate toward others? Are we as charitable or willing to share our resources with others as we can be – especially with the poor and dispossessed? Do we need to change our attitude toward people we disagree with ideologically or politically? Do we still retain vestiges of racial, social, or ethnic prejudices that are based on nothing but worn-out stereotypes? With a certain focus on our "Church lives," can we begin to read the Scriptures with greater regularity? Or practice charity, prayer, and fasting with greater care? Finally, are we interested in becoming a decent human being that seeks to enrich the lives of others around us?

As St Paul wrote, "Now is the acceptable time" (2 Cor 6.2). Great Lent can become the beginning of the end of a way of life we need to abandon, and the "beginning of the beginning" of the acquisition of the virtues we desire to embrace and practice. All this may be realized through "the grace of our Lord Jesus Christ, the love of God [the Father], and the fellowship of the Holy Spirit" (2 Cor 13.14).

The First Monday of March
Originally Written: April 2014

On the Liturgy of St Basil the Great

During the five Sundays of Great Lent, we celebrate the Liturgy of St Basil the Great. This liturgy is used on five other occasions during the year, two of which are during Holy Week – Thursday and Saturday. (The other three times are the Feasts of Nativity and Theophany, and the Feast of St Basil on January 1.) This Liturgy is known for its longer prayers, which may challenge our capacity to stand still in concentration and prayerful attention. But *what prayers!* Personally, they strike me as unrivaled in their beauty of expression and the depth of their theological and spiritual content. Although we hear them in translation, that beauty and depth remain intact.

St Basil did not sit down and compose the entire Liturgy "from scratch," to use a common expression. The basic structure of the Liturgy was already an essential element of the Church's living liturgical tradition. However, there is every reason to believe that he is responsible for the magnificent Anaphora prayers. These prayers reflect St Basil's intense preoccupation with the Church's trinitarian faith – that we worship the one God as the Father, and the Son, and the Holy Spirit; the Son and the Holy Spirit being *consubstantial* with the Father as to their divine nature, and thus co-enthroned and co-glorified with the Father from all eternity. (St Basil wrote a separate, magnificent treatise *On the Holy Spirit*, demonstrating the divinity of the Holy Spirit through his knowledge of the Scriptures and the Church's liturgical tradition.) That belief in the Holy Trinity, though present "in the beginning" of the Church's proclamation of the Gospel, was under attack during the turbulent fourth century, with the Arian heresy and its various offshoots that stirred up seemingly interminable debate and dissension. St Basil was among the premier exponents of the Church's faith that the one God *is* the Holy Trinity. He helped establish the classical terminology of the Church in expressing that faith: God is one in "essence" (in Greek, *ousia*), yet three distinct "persons" (*hypostaseis*). That terminology remains intact to this day. The Anaphora Prayer (which begins: "O Existing One, Master, Lord God, Father almighty and adorable") is steeped in praise and glorification of the Father, Son, and Holy Spirit. It thus deserves our deepest attention and reverence as we stand in the presence of the Holy Trinity and as we join the angelic powers in the so-called Thrice-Holy Hymn, "singing, shouting, and proclaiming: Holy! Holy! Holy! Lord of Sabaoth!"

Concerning the prayers of the Liturgy that reveal the Church's belief in the Holy Trinity, we find St Basil's unrivaled expression of the divine "economy" (*oikonomia*) throughout. This refers to God's providential dispensation or design toward His creation – culminating in the salvation of the world – in and through the incarnation, death, resurrection, and glorification of Christ. If I were asked for the most succinct expression of the divine economy as proclaimed by the Orthodox Church, I would refer to the long Anaphora Prayer of St Basil's Liturgy beginning where the Thrice-Holy Hymn leaves off. After praising God "for the magnificence of Thy holiness," we begin to recall – and thus make present – the full extent of His providential dispensation toward the world: "When Thou didst create man by taking dust from the earth, and didst honor him with Thine own image, O God." This long remembrance takes us from the fall into sin, through the promises of the prophets ("foretelling to us the salvation which was to come") and to the incarnation, death, resurrection, ascension, and even second coming of Christ: "Ascending into heaven, He sat down at the right hand of Thy majesty on high, and He will come to render to every man according to his works."

Actualizing "the night in which He gave himself up for the life of the world," as the Second Prayer of the Anaphora phrases it, this entire process culminates in the *epiklesis*, or invocation, of the Holy Spirit, "to bless, to hallow, and to show" that the bread and wine of our offering are now the Body and Blood of our Lord God and Savior, Jesus Christ. We will then receive the holy gifts "for the remission of sins and unto life everlasting."

Today, the Orthodox faithful in many jurisdictions are blessed in that the prayers of St Basil's Liturgy generally are read aloud so that the entire gathered assembly of believers may truly "hear" the prayers that reveal the Lord God's trinitarian nature and the divine economy together with the consecration of the Holy Gifts. Indeed, for many centuries this may not have been so, and even today it is not so in all Orthodox churches. So, we thank God for our own liturgical revival which has so enlivened our contemporary worship experience with full parish participation in the Church at prayer and praise. However, and admittedly, there is one final prayer near the end of the Liturgy that is usually read as the choir is singing. As the priest faces the table of preparation, and as the choir sings "Blessed be the name of the Lord, henceforth and forevermore" three times, the priest prays:

> The mystery of Thy dispensation, O Christ our God, has been accomplished and perfected as far as it was in our power; for we have had the memorial of Thy death; we have seen the type of Thy Resurrection; we have been filled with Thine unending life; we have enjoyed Thine inexhaustible food; which in the world to come be well-pleased to vouchsafe to us all, through the grace of Thine eternal Father, and Thy holy and good and life-creating Spirit, now and ever and unto ages of ages. Amen.

This summation of the meaning, purpose, and experience of the Liturgy is an amazing claim that perhaps may strike us more effectively if we break the prayer down into its component parts:

- We have had the memorial of the Lord's death;
- We have seen the type of the Lord's resurrection;
- We have been filled with the Lord's unending life;
- We have enjoyed the Lord's inexhaustible food;
- We ask to continue this partaking in the world to come; and
- All this through the grace of the Father, the Son, and the Holy Spirit.

This certainly gives new meaning to the experience we so blandly describe as "going to church." Clearly the remainder of the day is all downhill – no matter what we do! When we begin the Liturgy of Saint Basil the Great, we know that we have a long road ahead of us. That will require some patience, concentration, and a willingness to persevere to its dismissal. If we can do that, the rewards are inestimable. It will also test our deepest desires concerning what is "the one thing needful" in our lives and what is the treasure of our hearts. Yet, the Sundays of Great Lent are a unique opportunity to further our movement toward the gladsome light of the kingdom of God.

The Second Monday of March
Originally Written: April 2013

To Refresh Our Souls and Encourage Us

Before Thy Cross, we bow down in worship, O Master, and Thy Holy Resurrection, we glorify.
(Troparion of the Cross)

The hymn above – together with the accompanying rite of venerating the cross – replaces the usual Trisagion Hymn during the Divine Liturgy on the third Sunday of Great Lent. According to the *Synaxarion of the Lenten Triodion and Pentecostarion*,* the full title of this mid-Lent commemoration is: "The Sunday of the Veneration of the Precious and Life-Giving Cross." In a wonderful commentary, the *Synaxarion* sets before our spiritual sight the meaning of this commemoration and its timing:

> The precious and Life-giving Cross is now placed before us to refresh our souls and encourage us who may be filled with a sense of bitterness, resentment, and depression. The Cross reminds us of the Passion of our Lord, and by presenting to us His example, it encourages us to follow Him in struggle and sacrifice, being refreshed, assured and comforted.**

Hopefully, the first three weeks of the Fast – even if we have truly "crucified the flesh with its passions and desires" (Gal 5.24) – have not led us to experience "bitterness, resentment, and depression." However, we could be suffering from precisely those spiritual

---

* A compendium of texts and short commentaries on the meaning of various commemorations during the seasons of Great Lent and Pascha.
** David Kidd, Gabriella Ursache, and Seraphim Dedes, eds., *Synaxarion: of the Lenten Triodion and Pentecostarion* (Rives Junction, MI: HDM Press, 1999), 78.

wounds for other reasons and diverse circumstances in our lives, both external and internal. My own pastoral experience tells me that that is probably – if not assuredly – the case. And there is no better time than Great Lent to acknowledge this. Doing so could lead to genuine healing if pursued in a patient and humble manner.

How, then, can we be healed? Perhaps the Sunday of the Cross reveals our basic starting point. The cross of our Lord, placed before our vision, can release us from our bondage to these passions when we realize that Christ transformed this instrument of pain, suffering and death into an emblem of victory. Christ has absorbed and taken our sins upon himself, nailing them to the cross. In the process, "He disarmed the principalities and powers and made a public example of them, triumphing over them in him" (Col 2.15). These "principalities and powers" continue to harass us to this day, but if we are "in Christ" we can actualize His victory over them and reveal their actual powerlessness. Our lenten journey is leading us to the foot of the cross and to the empty and life-giving tomb, and the third Sunday of Great Lent anticipates our final goal as an encouragement. Again, from the *Synaxarion*:

> As they who walk on a long and hard way are bowed down by fatigue find great relief and strengthening under the cool shade of a leafy tree, so do we find comfort, refreshment, and rejuvenation under the Life-giving Cross, which our holy Fathers "planted" on this Sunday. Thus, we are fortified and enabled to continue our Lenten journey with a light step, rested and encouraged.*

Certainly, none of the above is meant to deflect our attention away from the "scandal of the cross" by poeticizing this scandal away in pious rhetoric. We must never lose sight of the sufferings of our Lord and the price He paid to release us from bondage to sin and death. In its indifference, the world will never understand

---

* Ibid., 79.

the enormity of Christ's sacrifice. Martin Hengel reminds us of the utter horror of crucifixion as a form of capital punishment:

> Crucifixion satisfied the primitive lust for revenge and the sadistic cruelty of individual rulers and of the masses. It was usually associated with other forms of torture, including at least flogging. At relatively small expense and to great public effect the criminal could be tortured to death for days in an unspeakable way. Crucifixion is thus a specific expression of the inhumanity dormant within men which these days is expressed, for example, in the call for the death penalty, for popular justice and for harsher treatment of criminals, as an expression of retribution. It is a manifestation of trans-subjective evil, a form of execution which manifests the demonic character of human cruelty and bestiality.[*]

So much for the noble simplicity and greatness of the ancient world! But there is nothing new under the sun, and fallen human nature is just as cruel and evil today. Again, Christ absorbed that cruelty and bestiality on the cross. This was a scandal, for the Son of God died the death of a slave. Now, as a "new creation" in Christ, we must exercise our freedom from precisely that dark and demonic abyss into which human beings can plunge, while also manifesting the transfiguration of our human energy into the virtues so wonderfully revealed in the lives of the saints. This was the prayer of the Apostle Paul when the light of the crucified and risen Lord began to shine in a world of darkness:

> May you be strengthened with all power, according to his glorious might, for all endurance and patience with joy, giving thanks to the Father who has qualified us [or you] to share in the inheritance of the saints in light. He has delivered us from the dominion of darkness and transferred

---

[*] *Crucifixion: In the Ancient World and the Folly of the Message of the Cross*, trans. John Bowden (Philadelphia, PA: Fortress Press, 1977), 87.

us to the kingdom of his beloved Son, in whom we have redemption, the forgiveness of sins. (Col 1.11–14)

The Church understands and will put before our gaze the sufferings of the Lord during Holy Week. At the same time, it is from within the Church we come to know the victory of Christ achieved through His death on the cross and fully revealed in His resurrection. Thus, the marvelous paradox of venerating a "life-giving cross." The rhetoric of the Church is thereby not empty but revelatory of a mystery that has been accomplished in our midst. The *Synaxarion* concludes its entry for this Sunday with the following prayer – a fitting way to bring this meditation to a close:

> O Christ our God, through the power of the Holy Cross, deliver us from the influence of our crafty enemy and count us worthy to pass with courage through the course of the forty days and to venerate Your divine Passion and Your Life-giving Resurrection. Be merciful to us, for You alone are good and full of love for mankind. Amen.[*]

---

[*] Kidd, Ursache, and Dedes, eds., *Synaxarion*, 80.

The Third Monday of March
Originally Written: March 2013

The Announcement of the Incarnation

March 25 is the Feast of the Annunciation to the Most Holy Theotokos. This feast always falls during Great Lent. Even if it falls during the week, the Liturgy of Saint John Chrysostom is served, which is the only time a full eucharistic Liturgy is served on a weekday in Great Lent. Thus, the Annunciation is a festal interlude that punctuates the eucharistic austerity of the lenten season. Yet, because it does occur during Great Lent, this magnificent feast appears and disappears rather abruptly. Each year, we no sooner change the lenten colors in church to the characteristic blue of feasts dedicated to the Theotokos than we find ourselves changing the colors back again. This is so because the Leavetaking of the Annunciation is on March 26. If we are not alert, it can fly below our "spiritual radar."

This feast has its roots in the account in St Luke's Gospel, wherein the evangelist narrates the dialog between the angel Gabriel and the Virgin Mary (Lk 1.26–38). The angel Gabriel "announces" the joyful news of the impending birth of the Messiah, hence the feast being called "Annunciation" in English. However, the Greek title of *Evangelismos* is even richer in that it captures the truth that the Gospel – *evangelion* – is being "announced" in the encounter between God's messenger and the young maiden destined to be the Mother of God. Her "overshadowing" by the Holy Spirit is "good news" for her and for the entire world! Even though the Feast of the Lord's Nativity in the flesh dominates our ecclesial and cultural consciousness, it is this Feast of the Annunciation that reveals the *incarnation*, or the "becoming flesh" of the eternal Word of God. It is the Word's conception in the womb of the Virgin Mary that is the "moment" of the Word's enfleshment. Hence, the Church's insistence that a new human being begins to exist at the moment of conception. The Word made flesh – our Lord Jesus Christ – will be born nine months later (on December 25 according to our liturgical calendar); but again, His very conception is the beginning of His human life as God-made-man. The Troparion of the Feast captures this well:

> Today is the beginning of our salvation; the revelation of the eternal Mystery!
>
> The Son of God becomes the Son of the Virgin as Gabriel announces the coming of Grace.
>
> Together with him let us cry to the Theotokos: Rejoice, O Full of Grace, the Lord is with you.

Was the Virgin Mary randomly chosen for this awesome role? Was she compelled to fulfill the will of God regardless of her spiritual relationship with God? Was she a mere instrument overwhelmed or even "used" by God for the sake of God's eternal purpose? That the Virgin Mary was "hailed" as one "highly favored" or "full of grace" (*kecharitômenê*) when the angel Gabriel first descended to her, points us well beyond any such utilitarian role for her. On the contrary, the Annunciation to the Virgin Mary is understood and presented by the Church as the supreme example of *synergy* in the Holy Scriptures, a term that conveys a harmonious cooperation of divine grace and human freedom between God and human beings. God does not compel, but seeks our free cooperation to be "co-workers" with Him in the process of salvation and deification. In this way, God respects our human self-determination, or what we often refer to as free will. It was the Virgin Mary's free assent to accept the unique vocation that was chosen for her from all eternity that allowed her to become the Theotokos, or "God-bearer." This is reflected in her response to the angel Gabriel's announcement: "Behold, I am the handmaid of the Lord;

let it be to me according to your word" (Lk 1.38). This teaching on synergy finds its classical expression in a justifiably famous passage from St Nicholas Cabasilas' *Homily on the Annunciation*:

> The incarnation of the Word was not only the work of the Father, Son and Spirit – the first consenting, the second descending, and third overshadowing – but it was also the work of the will and faith of the Virgin. Without the three divine persons this design could not have been set in motion; but likewise the plan could not have been carried into effect without the consent and faith of the all-pure Virgin. Only after teaching and persuading her does God make her his Mother and receive from her the flesh which she consciously wills to offer him. Just as he was conceived by his own free choice, so in the same way she became his Mother voluntarily and with her free consent.

We praise the Virgin Mary as representing our longing for God and for fulfilling her destiny so that we may receive the gift of salvation from our Lord who "came down from heaven and was incarnate of the Holy Spirit and the Virgin Mary and became man" (*The Nicene Creed*):

> Hail, thou who art full of grace: the Lord is with thee.
> Hail, O pure Virgin; Hail, O Bride unwedded.
> Hail, Mother of life: blessed is the fruit of thy womb.
> (*Dogmatikon*, Vespers of the Annunciation)

The Fourth Monday of March
Originally Written: April 2016

The Real Stairway to Heaven

Led Zeppelin's "Stairway to Heaven," is a pop-culture fixture that is still widely recognized today, some forty-five years after it was first released. I, for one, will openly confess to seeing and hearing this song performed live more than once. I even recall reading that – until a certain date, at least – it was the most-played song in rock radio history, so much so that the members of Led Zeppelin grew tired of their famous song.

Admittedly, I always found the lyrics rather opaque and esoteric. But if the song itself fails to captivate us, the title is at least worthy of attention. It awakens a vague longing deep within the human soul: Is there a "stairway to heaven"? Some sort of path to another reality that lifts us above the mundane and quotidian cares of life? Was there some formula hidden within the song's lyrics that pointed to that alluring path?

On the Fourth Sunday of Great Lent we commemorate a saint whose spiritual classic I often refer to as the *real* "stairway to heaven." That saint is St John Climacus († 649), austere author of the famous treatise *The Ladder of Divine Ascent*. St John was inspired by the vision of the Patriarch Jacob, who saw a ladder stretching from earth to heaven, upon which "the angels of God were ascending and descending" (Gen 28.12), the same vision Christ referred to in John 1. In *The Ladder*, St John develops this image as an effective teaching tool:

> His ladder has thirty rungs or steps, one for each year in the hidden life of Christ before His baptism. John's ingenious use of the ladder-image soon became part of

the spiritual imagination of the Christian East, and is frequently represented in panel icons, refectory frescoes and illuminated manuscripts.*

More than a millennium since its inception, Christians continue to read *The Ladder* with seriousness and devotion as a guide to the kingdom of heaven. As Kallistos Ware writes:

> With the exception of the Bible and the service books, there is no work in Eastern Christendom that has been studied, copied and translated more often than *The Ladder of Divine Ascent* by St. John Climacus.
>
> Every Lent in Orthodox monasteries it is appointed to be read aloud in church or in the refectory, so that the monks will have listened to it as much as fifty or sixty times in the course of their life.
>
> Outside the monasteries it has also been the favorite reading of countless lay people in Greece, Bulgaria, Serbia, Russia, and throughout the Orthodox world. The popularity of *The Ladder* in the East equals that of *The Imitation of Christ* in the West, although the two books are altogether different in character.**

This great abbot of Mount Sinai described with clarity and depth the interior "withdrawal" from worldliness; the struggle with the passions; the acquisition of the virtues; and the final ascent of the soul into the realm where faith, hope, and love prepare the believer for the incomprehensible glory yet to be experienced when God will be "all in all":

> Love, by its nature, is a resemblance of God, insofar as this is humanly possible. In its activity it is inebriation of

---

* Kallistos Ware, "Introduction," in *John Climacus: The Ladder of Divine Ascent*, eds. Colm Lubheid and Norman Russel (New York, NY: Paulist Press, 1988), 1-70, here 11.
** Ware, "Introduction," 1.

> the soul. Its distinctive character is to be a fountain of faith, an abyss of patience, a sea of humility.... Love grants prophecy, miracles. It is an abyss of illumination, a fountain of fire, bubbling up to inflame the thirsty soul. It is the condition of angels, and the progress of eternity.[*]

St John's work clearly bespeaks the monastic milieu from which it emerged. Nonetheless, since those very passions that plague us remain unchanging – and since the very virtues we struggle to acquire also remain unchanging – his writings have a timeless and eternal quality to them. Such a text is never really "dated" and does not belong to any fleeting movement or fad. *The Ladder* is an enduring monument of spiritual depth that flows from the Gospel. Indeed, there is an extraordinary passage in "Step One" that so beautifully captures the meaning of the Gospel, and of God's love for His creation and creatures. This passage takes on even greater poignancy when we recall that St John was fiercely ascetical and at times impatient with false teaching. But here he is truly expansive and He embraces all of humankind:

> God is the life of all free beings. He is the salvation of believers and unbelievers, of the just or the unjust... of monks or those living in the world, of the educated or the illiterate, of the healthy or the sick, of the young or the very old. He is like the outpouring of light, the glimpse of the sun, or the changes of the weather, which are the same for everyone without exception. "For God is no respecter of persons" (Rom. 2:11).[**]

Although employing what are essentially identical images, I believe that we can say with real assurance that *The Ladder of Divine Ascent* is on much firmer ground and has greater staying power than whatever is the endpoint of "Stairway to Heaven." In fact, I may be reproached for even making the comparison! Yet the association of images, and further reflection on the surrounding "culture"

---

[*] Lubheid and Russel, eds., *John Climacus*, 286.
[**] Ibid., 74.

that produced each work – and that is embodied within each work – come to mind as we move into the fourth week of Great Lent.

In our postmodern age of changeable narratives, there is nothing quite like the "rock" on which the Gospel is firmly planted. Other enticements built on the shifting sands of impermanence are swept away by time (Mt 7.24–27). St John built his house on the Gospel and thus continues to nourish us to this day with his wise counsel:

> Baptized in the thirtieth year of His earthly age, Christ attained the thirtieth step on the spiritual ladder, for God indeed is love, and to Him be praise, dominion, power. In Him is the cause, past, present, and future, of all that is good forever and ever. Amen.[*]

---

[*] Ibid., 291.

The First Monday of April
Originally Written: March 2014

Acedia, Us, and Our Lenten Effort

My soul, my soul arise! Why are you sleeping? The end is approaching and you will be confounded. Awake then, and be watchful, that you may be spared by Christ God, Who is everywhere and fills all things. (*Kontakion*, Great Canon of St Andrew of Crete)

Great Lent is a time for the soul to awaken from the sleep of sin, or from sheer indifference and apathy – what the saints call *acedia* – a condition of spiritual torpor or unsatisfied restlessness. This Great Lent, I am (finally) beginning to read a book I've had in my library for quite a while: *Acedia & Me: A Marriage, Monks and a Writer's Life*.* The author, Kathleen Norris, has developed a reputation as an insightful writer on religious themes through such books as *Dakota: A Spiritual Biography* and *The Cloister Walk*, to name just two of her more prominent titles. (She also has a book with the intriguing title, *The Quotidian Mysteries: Laundry, Liturgy and "Women's Work,"* a series of lectures based on discovering the sacred in what are considered mundane domestic chores.) Her career began as a poet, and she is now an oblate (or lay affiliate) of the Assumption Abbey in North Dakota. Her books trace her growing Christian faith and her contact with certain Roman Catholic monastic communities in North America.

In *Acedia & Me*, she has chosen to write about the "passion" of *acedia* in a contemporary setting and its almost universal affliction of the "modern" person, usually as the condition that we now call depression – a rather Orthodox theme, to be sure. This passion was discovered and written about in the earliest years of

---

* (New York: Riverhead Books, 2010).

the monastic movement by the desert fathers, who analyzed this passion and offered guidance on how to overcome it. This was the "noonday demon" mentioned in the Psalms and with whom the desert ascetics had to do battle before they could grow spiritually. Among the most famous descriptions of this passion is one found in the writings of Evagrius of Pontus (345-399):

> The demon of *acedia* – also called the noonday demon – is the one that causes the most serious trouble of all. He presses his attack upon the monk about the fourth hour and besieges the soul until the eighth hour. First of all he makes it seem that the sun barely moves, if at all, and that the day is fifty hours long. Then he constrains the monk to look constantly out the windows, to walk outside the cell, to gaze carefully at the sun to determine how far it stands from the ninth hour [or lunchtime], to look this way and now that to see if perhaps [one of the brethren appears from his cell]. Then too he instills in the heart of the monk a hatred for the place, a hatred for his very life itself, a hatred for manual labor. He leads him to reflect that charity has departed from among the brethren, that there is no one to give encouragement.... No other demon follows close upon the heals of this one (when he is defeated) but only a state of deep peace and inexpressible joy arise out of this struggle.[*]

Evagrius understood that this demon tempts the monk with the "unsatisfied restlessness" described above. Here we find boredom, tedium, restlessness, impatience, and a lack of care, all making prayer undesirable and impossible. In this condition, we are seemingly overwhelmed by the futility of our efforts. Evagrius' point is that this spiritual malaise drives the ascetic – and the layperson – to distraction. No wonder that this passage is so often quoted today; it remains a penetrating psychological and spiritual analysis of a malady that easily translates from the world of the desert ascetics

---

[*] Evagrius, *Praktikos* 12, quoted in Norris, *Acedia & Me*.

to the world that we know and live in today. In fact, Norris writes the following about the passage from Evagrius: "As I read this I felt a weight lift from my soul, for I had just discovered an accurate description of something that had plagued me for years but that I had never been able to name."[*]

Norris begins her book by relating modern definitions of the word *acedia*, which has remained in our vocabulary over the centuries, though not readily used:

> The ancient word *acedia*, which in Greek simply means the absence or lack of care, has proved anything but simple when it comes to finding adequate expression in English. Modern writers tend to leave the term untranslated, or employ the later Latin *accedie*. A few examples may help the reader comprehend the broad range of meaning of the word, as it is currently understood.

The *Oxford English Dictionary* (1989), defines *acedia* as "heedlessness, torpor, a non-caring state," while *Webster's Third New International Dictionary of the English Language* (1976), describes it as "anxiety, grief, the deadly sin of sloth, spiritual torpor and apathy." And, according to the *Online Medical Dictionary* (2000), *acedia* is "a mental syndrome, the chief features of which are listlessness, carelessness, apathy, and melancholia." Norris roots this condition – ever-present in modern life – to the same sickness Evagrius spoke of (above). As she puts it, it is likely "that much of the restless boredom, frantic escapism, commitment phobia, and enervating despair that plagues us today is the ancient demon of *acedia* in modern dress."[**]

Her book rightly indicates that *acedia* in the original Greek (usually spelled *akedía*) literally means "lack of care." Yet it is helpful to understand the simple but deep term "care" that we readily use. Here again, is a probing point from Norris:

[*] Norris, *Acedia & Me*, 4.
[**] Ibid., 3.

> That it hurts to care is borne out in etymology, for care derives from an Indo-European word meaning "to cry out," as in a lament. Caring is not passive, but an assertion that no matter how strained and messy our relationships can be, it is worth something to be present, with others, doing our small part.[*]

In closing her opening chapter, Kathleen Norris offers a summary of what I would imagine are themes the book in its totality may explore: "I have come to believe that *acedia* can strike anyone whose work requires self-motivation and solitude, anyone who remains married 'for better for worse,' anyone determined to stay true to a commitment that is sorely tested in everyday life."[**] And I wonder: Do we stay so busy in order to unconsciously flee from the noonday demon of *acedia*? Do we fill up our time and our lives with endless activity because we feel that dreadful *acedia* creeping up on us? Or is it the *acedia* that drives us forward so restlessly to always doing something – anything – because we no longer have the ability to be still, to truly "rest" in God as the saints described a life of prayer and stillness/*hesychia*?

The prayer of St Ephraim – the quintessential lenten prayer of the Church, so deeply focused as in the Canon of Repentance of St Andrew of Crete, is one weapon that we must employ in our battle with the "demon" of *acedia* and other forms of spiritual torpor and apathy. In the darkened and prayerful atmosphere in the Church that signifies the lenten season, we can concentrate and be still, at least to some extent, as the moving words of repentance and compunction move over us and plant themselves in our hungry and thirsty souls – souls that can only be filled by God. We have a sure hope in the Church that the noonday demon of *acedia* can be overcome and expelled from our lives. If we cooperate with God – that is, practice synergy – then we enter the realm where the impossible becomes possible as Christ promised us (cf. Mt 19.26).

---

[*] Ibid., 3-4.
[**] Ibid., 6.

The Second Monday of April
Originally Written: April 2016

Holy Week: A Mystic Torrent

As we enter Holy Week, the festal atmosphere of Lazarus Saturday and Palm Sunday yields to the solemnity, sobriety, and sadness of Holy Week as the Lord moves toward His voluntary and life-giving passion. The Son of God came into the world "to bear witness to the truth" (Jn 18.37) and "to give his life as a ransom for many" (Mk 10.45). It is our privilege and responsibility to accompany Christ to Golgotha to the extent that our lives make that possible, especially by our participation in the services that guide us to Golgotha and beyond – to the empty tomb. As Fr Sergius Bulgakov wrote, "The beauty, the richness and the power of these services take possession of the soul and sweep it along as upon a mystic torrent."* Therefore, during Holy Week we are challenged to "lay aside all earthly cares" and focus on our Lord Jesus Christ, whether we are at a service or not. This is a week filled with school, church, and other necessary responsibilities. There is no room or time for worldly entertainment – not when the Lamb of God will be slain for the sins of the world.

At the services of Holy Week, we enter the "today" of the events being reactualized so that the event and all its salvific power is made present to the gathered community. Thus, we are not simply commemorating a past event for its dramatic impact, or presenting something of an Orthodox "passion play." Rather, we re-*present* the event of the Crucifixion so that we participate in it within the liturgical time of the Church's worship. As Bishop Hilarion Alfeyev writes, "Each one of us receives Christ as our personal Savior, and so we each make our own all the events of Christ's life through

---

* *The Orthodox Church* (Crestwood, NY: St Vladimir's Seminary Press, 1988), 131.

personal experience, to whatever extent we can. The feast day is a realization here and now of an event that occurred once in time but is always happening outside time." And he adds, speaking of the great saints and their faith in the resurrection of Christ, "They lived... by their experience of eternity and knew that Easter was not a single day of the year, but an eternal reality in which they participated daily."[*]

That means that our presence at one of the Holy Week services confronts us with a series of choices and decisions, as it did the original participants: to be with Christ or to be with any of those who chose to crucify Him. Will our lives reveal us as imitators of the sinful but repentant woman, or as imitators of Judas the betrayer? Do we show signs of repentance or do we betray Christ in the small events of daily living? Or, perhaps like those for whom a moment of decision was at hand, we remain "guiltless" but apathetic bystanders whose very indecisiveness keeps us distant from the company of Christ. This is essential to bear in mind precisely because we are referring to actual, concrete historical events that occurred at a particular place in time among a specific people – the Jews to whom Christ belonged and the Roman authorities that controlled much of Palestine. In our piety, we can inadvertently stand aloof of the actual *dramatis personae* caught up in the divine-human drama of our Lord's passion and harshly judge all of the "wrongdoers" from the safe distance of our Christian faith. However, if this blinds us to our own moral failings and weaknesses, then we undermine and subvert that very piety that we bring to the services. And we misunderstand the nature of the hymnography, which is meant to challenge us today as well as recall the events of the past that have shaped our faith in Christ.

Opinions may vary here, but I believe this to be especially true in our pluralistic society when it comes to the harshness with which

---

[*] *The Mystery of Faith: An Introduction to the Teaching and Spirituality of the Orthodox Church* (Crestwood, NY: St Vladimir's Seminary Press, 2002), 119.

"the Jews" are treated in some of our Holy Week hymnography. I believe that at least a few of the hymns stray into a dangerous area that today would be labeled "anti-Semitic." (This phrase is tossed about carelessly at times, but it also calls for our vigilance as Christians never to embrace the reality expressed therein.) If the Orthodox Church were better known, some of this hymnography would be brought to our attention in a challenging and critical manner. Certain Jews who were contemporaries of Christ – notably the Sanhedrin or "religious authorities" – condemned the Lord as a false Messiah, and with the connivance of Roman power, had Him crucified. This is historically true. However, the Sanhedrin represents "institutional religion" in its more unattractive guise – self-defensive and self-protective, putting the institution before the Truth and guarding the status quo when challenged from without by an authentic voice that comes from God. We witness this today in all forms of "institutional religion" within the various Christian traditions, including our own. As we contemplate the harsh realities of a fallen and sinful world that is even capable of putting Christ to death, we need to mourn human corruption as it even tempts us within our institutions and within our hearts today. Would any one of us have stepped forward to defend Christ when He was unjustly condemned, or would our own passivity and fear have left Him just as alone and isolated today as during the end of His earthly ministry?

Yet, God was "working" throughout this unbearable human drama to fulfill His will for our eternal salvation. Christ was not the victim of an unjust verdict, but the victor who was fulfilling His vocation as the Suffering Servant who would be vindicated by His Father following His crucifixion and death. As St Peter was forgiven his weakness and restored to fellowship with his Lord, so are we today, by the grace of God so abundantly poured out on us through Christ Jesus our Lord.

The Third Monday of April
Originally Written: April 2010

The Resurrection of Christ and the Rise of Christianity

Orthodox Christians believe that the New Testament Church and the Christian faith itself appeared at a specific point in history because the crucified Jesus of Nazareth was raised from the dead. The origin of the Church and the Christian faith was not a crucified, dead, and buried Jesus. Rather, that very crucified, dead and buried Jesus was revealed to be both Lord and Christ following His resurrection "on the third day." God vindicated the messianic claims of Jesus when He raised Jesus from the dead "according to the Scriptures." Contemporary Orthodox Christians readily agree with the Apostle Paul's insistence on the absolute centrality of the bodily resurrection of Christ as the foundation of Christian faith in Jesus: "If Christ is not raised, then your faith is in vain and our preaching is in vain" (1 Cor 15.14). This has been an overwhelming consensus among Christians since the initial witness of the apostles to the risen Lord.

But since the emergence of critical biblical scholarship within the last two centuries or so, we find Christian scholars and those influenced by them questioning, reinterpreting, or openly denying the bodily resurrection of Jesus. This process may be more accelerated today, or simply more prominent and public in its expression. A vivid – if not lurid – expression of this skeptical approach to the resurrection claims of the first Christians can be found in the work of the New Testament scholar Dom Dominic Crossan. In his reconstruction of events, the body of the crucified Jesus was discarded in a shallow grave to suffer the further humiliation of becoming the food of ravenous dogs. Incidentally, this is precisely the kind of counter-claim that attracts publicity. This threatens to undermine a consistent and long-standing witness among all Christians that points to the uniqueness of Jesus Christ among the great so-called "religious founders" of history. That uniqueness was articulated by Veselin Kesich in the following manner in his book *The First Day of the New Creation*:

> For the members of the first Christian community in Jerusalem, the resurrection of Christ was above all an event in the life of their Master, and then also in their own lives. After meeting Christ following his resurrection, they could have said with St. Paul that necessity was laid upon them to preach the gospel of resurrection (1 Cor. 9:16). Christianity spread throughout the Greco-Roman world with the proclamation that Jesus who died on the cross was raised to a new life by God. The message of Christianity is without parallel in religious history in its content and in its demand.[*]

The risen Christ spoke to His disciples about "belief" in His resurrection even among those who did not "see" Him as those very first disciples did. This was in response to the Apostle Thomas' movement from unbelief to belief when Jesus appeared to Thomas and allowed him to probe the wounds in His hands and side: "You have believed because you have seen me. Blessed are those who have not seen and yet believe" (Jn 20.29). Clearly, the presence of faith is essential in confessing that Jesus has been raised from the dead: "If you confess with your lips that Jesus is Lord and believe in your heart that God raised him from the dead, you will be saved" (Rom 10.9). However, in perhaps challenging a misconceived understanding of faith, this does not mean that believing that Jesus was bodily raised from the dead is an irrational leap into the unbelievable and indefensible.

On the one hand, the resurrection is an overwhelming and awesome event that evokes trembling and astonishment in those who

---

[*] (Crestwood, NY: St Vladimir's Seminary Press, 1997), 15.

are presented with its reality – and perhaps initial silence because of its numinous quality (see Mk 16.8). On the other hand, Christians do not believe in the resurrection of Christ in the face of evidence that clearly contradicts or "disproves" that claim. It is not as if the first disciples of Jesus were confronted with His (rotting) corpse in the tomb, but then said: "Nevertheless, we still believe that He is risen!" The resurrection of Christ is not about the fate of the "immortal soul" of Jesus, which is quite irrelevant to the Christian claim that death has been overcome in the resurrected Christ. Resurrection is the claim that the body – and thus the whole person conceived biblically – has been raised and glorified to a new mode of existence in an eternal relationship with God. What many Jews believed would occur at the end of history, happened with Jesus *within* history. And that is why the Apostle Paul called Christ "the first fruits of those who have fallen asleep" (1 Cor 15.20).

While we "see" the risen Lord through the eyes of faith, we also claim that the historical investigation into the reliability of the evidence for the resurrection, narrated, and developed in the New Testament, cannot refute that belief in any way. In Christianity, there exists a mutual interpenetration between theology and history. Thus, theology and history remain in an unbreakable bond of mutual support and clarification. Basically, Christians cannot make theological claims that are historically untenable or refutable. This is due to the foundational claim that God acts decisively on behalf of humankind and the world within the historical space and time of our created world. With this in mind, we can say that there are three essential components to the New Testament's proclamation of the resurrection of Jesus Christ that together present a reasonable defense of that claim that is simultaneously consistent, coherent and convincing: 1) the discovery of the empty tomb; 2) the appearances of the risen Lord to His male and female disciples; and 3) the transformation of the disciples into the apostles who boldly proclaim the risen Christ to the world, and the beginning of the New Testament Church.

The Empty Tomb

Christians do not believe in the empty tomb. Yet Christians believe that the tomb of Jesus must have been empty for them to convincingly announce His resurrection from the dead. The empty tomb simply revealed the fact that something happened to the body of the crucified Jesus. The empty tomb needed to be interpreted. Not expecting the resurrection of her master, Mary Magdalene's first reaction was to seek a "natural" interpretation for the empty tomb: "They have taken the Lord out of the tomb, and we do not know where they have laid him" (Jn 20.2). That the tomb of the dead Jesus was found empty on the "first day of the week," following His crucifixion and burial, is now universally acknowledged as a sound historical fact. Even scholars who do not believe in the resurrection of Christ accept the account of the burial of Jesus and the discovery of the empty tomb. The former Roman Catholic scholar, Geza Vermes, offers a good example of this basic consensus:

> When every argument has been considered and weighed, the only conclusion acceptable to the historian must be that the opinions of the orthodox, liberal sympathizer and the critical agnostic alike – and even perhaps of the disciples themselves – are simply interpretations of the one disconcerting fact: namely that the women who set out to pay their last respects to Jesus found to their consternation, not a body, but an empty tomb.[*]

And, of course, no one has ever claimed to have produced the corpse of Jesus. Whatever one may make of St Matthew's account (see 27.62–66), the Jewish propaganda concerning why the tomb of Jesus was discovered to be empty, presupposes the acceptance of the empty tomb in the first place. The counter-claim of the Jewish authorities – the "stolen" body of Jesus – was another appeal to a "natural" reason as to why the tomb was empty. But the

---

[*] *Jesus the Jew: A Historian's Reading of the Gospels* (London: Collins, 1973), 41.

appearance of the angel(s) within the tomb, recorded by all four evangelists, begins to point well beyond these natural explanations into the mysterious realm of God. For it is God who acted in both an unexpected and shatteringly decisive way by transforming the tomb into a womb from which emerges new and everlasting life. It was the women disciples of Jesus who first heard the Gospel of new life from within the tomb.

As prominent New Testaments scholars such as Raymond Brown, N.T. Wright, and William Lane Craig further point out, the discovery of the tomb by a group of women – the holy myrrh bearers – is a very convincing piece of evidence for the veracity of the canonical Gospels' account of the initial discovery of the empty tomb. This is because the witness of women was not binding according to the Law in first-century Judaism. The early Church would not have imaginatively given the privilege of discovering the empty tomb to witnesses who unfortunately were thought to be unreliable. In fact, according to Lk 24.11, the apostles initially thought that their words were "an idle tale." (Did the apostles ever get anything right until they saw the risen Lord and began to believe in Him?) With the proclamation of the angel from within the tomb, we are introduced into the good news which has changed the world once and for all: "Do not be amazed; you seek Jesus of Nazareth, who was crucified. He has risen, he is not here; see the place where they laid him. But go, tell his disciples and Peter that he is going before you to Galilee; there you will see him, as he told you" (Mk 16.6–7). This sets the stage for the appearances of the risen Christ to His disciples.

The Appearances of the Risen Lord

The appearances of the Risen Christ provide the needed interpretation to the empty tomb. The tomb is indeed empty because Jesus has been raised from the dead as the angel proclaimed. This is the dawn of the "new creation" and the "death of death." Each

Gospel ends with at least one chapter (two in the case of St John's Gospel) narrating one or more appearances of the risen Lord to His female and male disciples. These appearances initially overwhelmed the disciples and we hear of different reactions: "gladness" (Jn 20.20), "worship" and even "doubt" (Mt 28.17). In a marvelous expression in St Luke's Gospel, we even hear that the disciples "disbelieved for joy!" (Lk 24.41). There is also an initial non-recognition in some accounts (Lk 24.16; Jn 20.14).

The sheer unexpectedness of the crucified, but now risen Lord, appearing to His disciples must account for some of these various reactions. Yet, regardless of these initial reactions, the disciples are completely convinced that it is Jesus raised to new life and now in their midst as their "Lord and God" (Jn 20.28). From our vantage point today, it is virtually impossible for us to comprehend this experience of the first disciples of Christ. The resurrection was (and remains) a mysterious, unprecedented, and eschatological event. Perhaps this is what accounts for the lack of that narrative flow and continuity that we encounter in the narrative of the suffering, death and burial of Christ. The evangelists were hard-pressed to relate "the unrelatable" within the confines of our human language and images. At times, it seems as if language itself breaks down in its struggle to narrate the events of the appearances of Christ.

We discover in the risen Lord both continuity and discontinuity. It is the crucified, dead, and buried Jesus himself who is raised from the dead ("You seek Jesus of Nazareth"), a fact borne out by His still visible wounds (Jn 20.20, 27); and that He even takes food together with His disciples (Lk 24.42). Yet there is also a great deal of transformation in the risen Lord: He appears and disappears at will and closed doors are not obstacles to those appearances (Jn 20:19, 26; Lk 24:31). St Mark even informs us that He appeared "in another form" (Mk 16.12). When we consider the complementary aspects of continuity and discontinuity revealed in the risen Lord, then to speak of His "physical" resurrection can be misleading and open to skeptical dismissal.

This is because a "physical" resurrection can be misconstrued as a "mere" resuscitation – and hence resumption – of earthly existence as we experience it in the here and now of this world. And that was the case when Jesus raised to life the daughter of Jairus, the son of the widow of Cain, and His dear friend Lazarus. They all died again, after being brought back to life by the restorative power of Christ. The Lord, however, was resurrected to undying and eternal life: "For we know that Christ being raised from the dead will never die again; death no longer has dominion over him" (Rom 6.9).

For this reason, it is biblically sound to describe the resurrection as a "bodily" – rather than a strictly "physical" – event. Doing so distinguishes the resurrection of Christ from mere resuscitation. The term "bodily" also affirms the transformation that occurs in the resurrection, for the Lord is raised from death in a "spiritual body" according to the theologically-nuanced expression of the Apostle Paul (1 Cor 15.42–50). Raised to life in a spiritual body, the risen Lord reveals to us the glorified life of the age to come. In theological language, we refer to this as an "eschatological reality." This means that the hope we hold onto for the end of history – the fulfillment of God's design for the world – is already open to our experience within the here and now of history. And by grace, we will share this with the Lord in "the life of the world to come."

What is being stressed here, however, is that the disciples know that it is Jesus once they see Him following His resurrection. This is all summed up by St Luke in the second volume of his narrative history of Christ's ministry and the beginning of the Church's existence: "To them he presented himself alive after his passion by many proofs, appearing to them during forty days, and speaking of the kingdom of God" (Acts 1.3).

The Transformation of the Disciples and the Beginning of the New Testament Church

Something has to account for the evident transformation of Christ's disciples. They are portrayed in the Gospels in a painfully unflattering manner, based not only on their obtuseness during the ministry of Christ, but also on their cowardly failing to remain with Him in the hour of His suffering and death. They literally abandoned their master, and Peter openly denied even knowing Him. But in a very short span of time, those very disciples were transformed into apostles who would carry the Gospel to the "ends of the earth."

At the very heart of that Gospel was that Jesus had overcome death itself by His resurrection, thus inaugurating a new creation and the promise of eternal life with God: "But God raised him up, having loosed the pangs of death, because it was not possible for him to be held by it" (Acts 2:24). Crushed by the brutal and "cursed" death of their Master, and together with Him of their hope that Jesus was the Messiah; fearful and hiding behind closed doors "for fear of the Jews" (Jn 20.19); the messianic movement centered in Jesus was as dead as He apparently was lying in the tomb. A crucified, dead, and buried Messiah was not only meaningless, but completely incoherent from the Jewish perspective.

Something of great significance must have happened to make any sense of the disciples' newfound faith, boldness, and willingness to give their own lives for what they would proclaim to the world. Conspiracies or collective hallucinations are inept explanations that are now treated as more-or-less eccentric theories. These skeptical theories "disprove" nothing, but rather "prove" that it is very difficult to refute the plausibility of the Resurrection.

In their desire to maintain objectivity, but also to make some sense of the evidence provided to them, historians and scholars must face this historically unprecedented and baffling mystery of the origins of the Christian movement. For all the "data" tells us that this movement should never have even started. When they carefully examine the evidence and attempt to arrive at some conclusions concerning the cause of this new faith centered on Jesus of Nazareth – a condemned criminal put to death by the authority of the Roman Empire in the relatively remote and insignificant area of first century Judea – these very historians and scholars must provide a convincing alternative theory if they are not willing to accept the claim that Jesus was raised from the dead.

A fair question then forms itself naturally: considering the beliefs of first-century Judaism concerning the possibility of a crucified messiah, issues of "life after death," and the Jewish belief in the resurrection from the dead at the end of time; just how convincing are any of those alternative theories? Perhaps that is why some major New Testament scholars (such as E.P. Sanders), without committing themselves to an active faith in the resurrection of Christ, at least concede that the disciples of Christ were convinced they saw Him alive following His death on the cross. And that they then acted on that conviction.

To return to an initial point, I do not believe that Christians should base faith in Christ simply on carefully gathered evidence concerning Christ's resurrection from the dead. This is not a courtroom trial, and Christian faith is not based upon the "jury's" verdict. A commitment to Christ as the crucified and risen one (who has "trampled down death by death and upon those in the tombs bestowing life") begins with faith, which is based on trusting the witness of the apostles of Christ – *a witness that they were prepared to die for.* This trust slowly transforms each Christian so that that faith becomes living and personal. As that faith matures, all Christians may reach a point when they make their own the words of the Apostle Paul: "I have been crucified with Christ; it is no longer I who live, but Christ who lives in me; and the life I now live in the flesh I live by faith in the Son of God, who loved me and gave himself for me" (Gal 2.20).

Yet, the Christian claim is that God acts within human history. That God enters the time and space of our world to create, sustain, and redeem us as the Lord of history who has prepared a glorious future for us. The ultimate manifestation of that divine activity within the world is revealed in the incarnation of the eternal Son of God. And His death and resurrection from the dead fulfill the promises of God as He remains faithful to His faithless people throughout history. This historical aspect of our Christian faith means, to repeat this once more, that any historical evidence that can disprove the resurrection of Christ would immediately and definitively undermine that faith. But no such evidence exists. On the contrary, it points us toward the genuineness and authenticity of those very claims – as incredible and "unbelievable" as they may initially appear to be.

The Fourth Monday of April
Originally Written: May 2017

Paschal Reminiscences

While preparing for the priesthood, I was ordained as a deacon of the Church for my last three months at St Vladimir's Orthodox Seminary in New York (1981). I was thus able to serve together with Frs Alexander Schmemann, John Meyendorff, and Thomas Hopko, as well as with others in the "old chapel" during that brief period. That alone remains a memorable experience. This also meant serving as a deacon during Great Lent, Holy Week, and Pascha my final year at St Vladimir's. In the late morning of Pascha Sunday, Presvytera Deborah and I arrived early as we were gathering at the chapel for the Agape Vespers to be served at noon. Before the service began, I found myself standing on the porch of the chapel and looking out, absorbing the wonderful day – calm, cloudless, and mild, the sun shining brightly – and the array of colorful flowers and teeming bushes that adorned the chapel. The exhaustion of the previous Holy Week and the long paschal Liturgy earlier that morning seemed to momentarily disappear. Fr Schmemann joined me, dressed in his white paschal cassock, and clearly enjoying this "perfect day." After a bit of silence, he said something that has always stayed with me. Now, for some reason, there were times when he would not call me by my first name, but would address me in his French-Russian accented as "Kostoff." This was meant in a friendly, not a formal way. On this occasion, he leaned over and said, "Kostoff, it is a day like today that makes life meaningful." This was a typical example of Fr Schmemann's use of understatement. He thoroughly disliked pious rhetoric, long-winded theological conversations – "teaching God," he would bitingly say – and he was equally impatient with sentimentality.

Thus, all he needed to say was that this beautiful Pascha Sunday made life meaningful. These words were about Christ and His victory over death in His resurrection. That is what makes life meaningful. We had just completed our annual celebration of that life-creating victory, culminating hours earlier in the joyous midnight paschal Liturgy which we served together. The beauty of the day simply enhanced the life-changing meaning of the resurrection of Christ. Fr Schmemann was a thorough realist. He harbored no illusions about the destructive power of sin and the tragedy of history and life filled with sin. And, of course, there is death itself, overshadowing and undermining our quest for the "meaning of life." Fr Schmemann was implying, however, that without Christ's victory over sin and death, one is hard-pressed to find ultimate meaning in life. Or that all such attempts pale before the tangible reality of the risen Christ. That is how I understood his statement "it is a day like today that makes life meaningful." I like to think that it was our shared "worldview" and our joint membership in the Church that instantly revealed to me what he was conveying to me with this understated remark that came to him naturally – there was no need to "spell it out." It was a shared understanding. I do not recall how I responded, if I did at all. I am hoping that I merely nodded in agreement without trying to respond with something clever – why spoil the moment? We were eventually joined by a host of other priests and deacons (one of whom was Fr John Meyendorff, the brilliant Church historian and Patristics scholar), and someone offered to take a photograph of us all in front of the old chapel. I have this photo to this day and look at it periodically with fond nostalgia. By the following year, after I had graduated, the new chapel was in place.

To add another reminiscence from that same celebration of Pascha, I would share that during the earlier midnight Liturgy, while we had been in the sanctuary, Fr Schmemann leaned over and said to me, "Kostoff, a logical positivist could never understand all of this." It was an interesting comment to make in the middle of the

Liturgy. For Fr Schmemann, a "logical positivist" would have a truncated understanding of life precisely because he was trying to understand everything through the categories of logical thought. Yet life, in all its manifestations and beauty – as well as in its imperfections and irrationality – is far greater than logic. (The personal tragedy of placing logic above life was one of the major themes pursued by Dostoevsky with great penetration in his later novels.) At least that is how Fr Schmemann would see things, and I would fully agree with him. It is hard to work God into the structure of thought pursued by the logical positivist. Thus, the Christian revelation remains foreign, if not incoherent, to such a way of thinking. I am sure that that was implied in Fr Schmemann's quick aside to me in the sanctuary. But I believe that there was more.

The paschal Liturgy, as the culmination of the long and emotionally draining experience of Holy Week, is something like an "explosion of joy." There is something "childlike" in all the movement and singing: the procession, the initial proclamation that "Christ is Risen!" followed by the joyous singing of the Paschal Canon, "Let God Arise," and "The Angel Cried." The paschal services have meaningful structure, but formality and stuffy solemnity are abandoned in the acknowledgement and experience of the presence of the risen Lord. In all of this, we transcend the merely logical; not that what we are doing is "illogical," but the experience of paschal joy carries us to another level of reality. I believe Fr Schmemann was saying that this paschal exuberance escapes the narrow limitations of the "logical positivist." And I am glad he shared another memorable thought with me at that very moment. He realized that what we were doing would seem like foolishness to others, but that is beside the point. Without joy, Christianity is reduced to moral prescriptions and proscriptions. In fact, Fr Schmemann would often quote the German philosopher, Nietzsche, who would reproach Christians for having no joy, pointing out that a joyless Christianity was a contradiction in terms and unworthy of the attention of others.

It was an unforgettable experience to serve with – or simply to be around – Fr Alexander Schmemann. Delivered *ex tempore*, yet in his inimitable style, his somewhat pithy statements expressed the truth that a "meaningful life" is now one informed by the resurrection of Christ; and that a "logical positivist" may just come up short in his understanding of life. This is all part of a worldview that was profoundly Christ-centered and ecclesial. For Fr Alexander, Pascha was the perfect setting not only for expressing, but for experiencing the fullness of a genuinely Christian worldview. It was an honor to know him.

The First Monday of May
Originally Written: April 2014

"Lent after Lent" and "Life after Pascha"

Recently, I posed a question to the faithful of our parish: Is there life after Pascha? Another question has formed in my mind this morning: Is there Lent after Lent? Before proceeding further, I need to clarify two points. First, I apologize if I unsettled anyone with the frightening prospect of *another* immediate lenten period. Second, I am not a "lent freak"! I ask this question simply to pose a challenge: is there anything spiritually fruitful that we began to do – or anything spiritually unfruitful that we ceased to do – during Great Lent that we can carry over with us into the paschal season and beyond? Are we able to establish some genuine consistency in our ecclesial lives? Surely this is one of the most important elements in nurturing a holistic approach to our faith. If I am not mistaken, a real temptation that exists after Great Lent is to return to "life as usual," as if Great Lent were at best a pious interlude during which we act more "religiously," and at worst a period of specific rules meant to be mechanically observed out of a sense of obligation. This undermines the whole reality of repentance at its core, and drives us back into the dubious practice of the religious compartmentalization of our lives. Great Lent is over – now what?

I am not sure how healthy it is to assess and analyze our lenten efforts. Great Lent is a "school of repentance," but this does not mean that we are to grade ourselves upon its completion. However, there are a few things we can ask ourselves.

- Did I practice prayer, charity, and fasting in a more responsible, regular, and consistent manner?

- Did I make a point of reading the Scriptures with the same care and consistency?

- Did I participate in the liturgical services with greater regularity?

- Did I watch over my language, and gestures, or my words and actions, on an overall basis with greater vigilance?

- Did I make a breakthrough in overcoming any specific "passions" or other manifestations of sinful living?

- Did I work on mending any broken relationships?

- Did I simply give more of myself to Christ?

- Did I come to love Christ even more as I prostrated myself in faith before His life-giving cross and tomb?

Then why not continue? Not to continue is to somehow fail to actualize in our lives the renewal and restoration of our human nature that definitively occurred through the cross and resurrection. Appropriating the fruits of Christ's redemptive death and life-giving resurrection is essential for our self-designation as Christians.

In other words, can we carry the spirit of Lent (and some of its practices) with us outside of Lent? In this way, we are no longer "keeping Lent" but simply practicing our faith with the vigilance it requires. We still must fast (on the appropriate days), pray, and give alms. We still need to nourish ourselves with the Holy Scriptures. We must continue to wage war against the passions that are always threatening to engulf us. We need to deepen our love for Christ so that this surpasses any other commitment in our lives. Otherwise, have we not doomed ourselves to being intense in the practice of our faith only for a short, predetermined length of time, and then paying "lip service" to, or offer token observance of, the Christian life until next year? In a rather unfortunate twist, Great Lent can work against us when we reduce it to such a limited purpose. Great Lent is the designated time of year meant to get us "back on track," to live more conscious Christian lives because certain circumstances and our weaknesses often work against us. It is the example rather than the exception if properly understood. In other areas of life, do we simply abandon good practices – in matters of health, let us say – because a designated period of testing or observing these good practices has come to an end?

This week may be a good time to reawaken to the glorious gift of life offered to us in the Church. After Bright Week, we will return to our usual pattern of fasting on Wednesdays and Fridays, as the initial glow of Pascha slowly recedes. I would suggest that the first Wednesday after Pascha may be one of the most difficult days of fasting in the entire year. It is hard to reestablish a discipline temporarily suspended with the paschal celebration. In many ways, we return to "life as usual," even in the Church, but this way of life is newly directed by the wisdom of the Church toward our salvation and as a witness to the world. Let us take the "best of Lent" and continue with it throughout the days of our lives.

"Lent after Lent" means that there is "Life after Pascha."

The Second Monday of May
Originally Written: May 2013

Death's Dominion Has Been Shattered!

The souls bound in the chains of hades, O Christ, seeing Thy compassion without measure, pressed onward to the light with joyful steps, praising the eternal Pascha.
(Matins, Paschal Canon of St John of Damascus)

The awesome mystery of the Lord's bodily resurrection from the dead was providentially kept hidden from human eyes. Although there were many eyewitnesses to the resurrected one, there were none of the actual "moment" of the resurrection. There was no access to the tomb until the stone had been rolled away and its emptiness revealed to the myrrhbearing women. The emptiness of the tomb was a "sign" of the resurrection of Christ; the angelic voice ("He has risen, he is not here") was the first announcement of the Gospel of the risen Lord, thus interpreting the sign. The Lord then appeared to both the myrrhbearing women and the disciples, fully affirming the meaning of the empty tomb and the angelic proclamation. Yet, to repeat, the "moment" of the resurrection remains inaccessible to human perception.

For this reason, artistic depictions of Christ emerging from the tomb, banner in hand, rising in a blinding light over the hapless and sprawling bodies of the guard, are "later" and inauthentic images of the resurrection, though they contain the truth that the "Lord is risen indeed!" In the Western artistic tradition, the most famous of such depictions is probably that of Matthias Grünewald. Such images have also become popular in Orthodox iconography over the centuries, as seen on processional banners, portable icons and walls. Once such images enter the Church, they stubbornly refuse to leave.

There do exist two authentic icons of the resurrection, one being of a more historical nature and the other theological. The historical icon of the resurrection is that of the myrrhbearing women gazing in wonder at the empty grave cloths of Christ lying in the tomb while an angel (or two) sits inside the tomb as recorded in the Gospels. This icon captures the startling moment when the myrrhbearers were overcome with "fear and trembling" at not seeing the body of the Lord in the tomb.

The theological icon is simply entitled the "Anastasis" or "Resurrection," and is also referred to as the "Descent into Hades." Here the victorious Christ, resplendent in white garments, cross in hand, is depicted shattering the gates of the biblical realm of the dead (*sheol* in Hebrew; *hades* in Greek; imprecisely translated as "hell"), decisively and forcefully grabbing Adam and Eve – representative of humanity and the righteous awaiting deliverance (cf. Heb 11.39–40) – by the hand and pulling them out of this darkened realm, restored to fellowship with God. As iconography and hymnography complement one another, a paschal hymn from the Vespers of Holy Saturday illuminates the meaning of this powerful icon:

> Today Hell cries out groaning:
> My power has been trampled upon.
> The Shepherd is crucified and Adam is raised.
> I have been deprived of those whom I ruled.
> Those whom I swallowed in my strength I have given up.
> He who was crucified has emptied the tombs.
> The power of death has been vanquished.
> Glory to Thy Cross and Resurrection, O Lord.

The fathers found a clear allusion of this descent into hades in a passage from 1 Peter:

> For Christ also died for sins once for all, the righteous for
> the unrighteous, that he might bring us to God, being put

to death in the flesh but made alive in the spirit; *in which he went and preached to the spirits in prison,* who formally did not obey.... For this is why the gospel was preached even to the dead, that though judged in the flesh like men, they might live in the spirit like God. (1 Pet 3.18–4.6)

In a very early text of the second century, known as *The Odes of Solomon,* we find a dramatic description of the profound theological truth of the "descent into hades":

> I opened the barred gates,
> I broke the iron locks,
> and the iron became red and turned to liquid before me;
> and nothing more was shut up,
> because I am the door for every being.
> I went to free the captives,
> they are mine and I abandon no one. (Ode 17)

> Hell saw me and it was defeated,
> Death released me and many with me.
> I was its gall and vinegar.
> I descended through death into hell,
> into its very depth.
> Death...was unable to behold my countenance.
> Of the dead I made a living assembly. (Ode 42)

In other words, "Death's dominion has been shattered," as is proclaimed in the first Resurrection Sticheron of Holy Saturday Vespers. Can Christianity survive without this being the ultimate "good news," that "through death he might destroy him who has the power of death, that is, the devil, and deliver all those who through fear of death were subject to lifelong bondage" (Heb 2.14–15)?

What of the non-resurrected Christ emerging from certain biblical scholars and other circles now demanding equal time in the popular press and visual media? Is this even remotely consistent with the full content of the New Testament? Does such a "Christ" truly inspire and offer hope to the hopeless? I would answer my own questions with a decisive "No!" However, the Apostle Paul reminds us that "all the promises of God find their Yes in him" (2 Cor 1.20). This "Yes" seems fully convincing when we acknowledge Christ as "the faithful witness, the firstborn of the dead, and the ruler of kings of the earth" (Rev 1.20).

Christ is risen! Indeed, He is risen!

The Third Monday of May
Originally Written: July 2015

"Do You Want to Be Healed?"

In the fifth chapter of the Gospel of St John, we find the account of the healing of the paralytic by the Pool of Bethesda near the sheep gate in Jerusalem and the profound discourse that follows. Archaeologists have recently discovered this pool, demonstrating the accuracy of St John's description. The paralytic had taken his place among a human throng of chronic misery, described by the evangelist as "a multitude of invalids, blind, lame, paralyzed" (Jn 5.3). Being there for 38 years and not being able to experience what were believed to be the healing capacities of the waters of the pool, the paralytic seemed resigned to his destiny. Then Jesus appeared. Seeing the paralytic and knowing of his plight, Jesus asked him a pointed question: "Do you want to be healed?" (v. 6). Surprisingly, considering what must have been his own misery, the paralytic's answer was less than direct and not exactly enthusiastic: "Sir, I have no man to put me into the pool when the water is troubled, and while I am going another steps down before me" (v. 7). Nevertheless, although the paralytic does not commit himself to an act of faith in the healing power of Jesus, he receives the following directive from Jesus: "Rise, take up your pallet, and walk." And then, in that somewhat laconic style of describing the healing power of Christ which characterizes the Gospel accounts, we read simply, "And at once the man was healed, and he took up his pallet and walked" (v. 9). The "sign" is that Christ can restore wholeness to those in need.

I believe we need to concentrate on the question Jesus posed to the paralytic: "Do you want to be healed?" (The King James Version of the question is: "Wilt thou be made whole?") In a way, the various characters Jesus encountered in the Gospels were representatives or "types" of certain human dilemmas or states of being. Jesus' question therefore remains alive in each generation and is posed to each of us today. If sin is a sickness, then we are "paralyzed" by that sin to one degree or another. But do we *really* want to be healed of the paralyzing effect of sin in our lives? The answer seems obvious at first glance, a "no-brainer," but is that truly the case? Or are we more content to continue as we are, satisfied that perhaps this is "as good as it gets" in terms of our relationship with God and our neighbor? Do we manage to politely deflect the probing question of Christ elsewhere, counter-posing a reasonable excuse as to what prevents us from exerting the necessary energy from our side? Our teaching claims that we must also contribute to the synergistic process of divine grace and human freedom that work together harmoniously for our healing. Perhaps it is easier and more comfortable to stay as we are (after all, it's not that bad – or so we rationalize), a position reflected in the non-committal response of the paralytic. For to be further healed of sin will mean that we will have to make some changes in our lives, in our interior attitudes, and in our relationships. It certainly means we will have to confess our faith in Christ with a greater intensity, urgency, and commitment. Are we up to that challenge?

More to the point, we could in fact say that we have already been healed. That happened when we were baptized into Christ. (There are baptismal allusions in the healing of the paralytic by the pool of water.) Every human person is paralyzed by the consequences of sin, distorting the image of God in which we were initially created. Baptism is meant to put to death the sin that is within us. We *were* healed, in that baptism is the pledge to life everlasting, where death itself is swallowed up in the victory of Christ over death. For we are baptized into the death and resurrection of Christ. With this in mind, Christ's perennial question to the paralytic ("Do you wish to be healed?") could be rephrased: Do you rejoice in the fact that you have been healed, and does your way of life reflect the faith and joy that that great healing from sin and death has imparted to you? Are you willing to continue in the struggle that is necessary to keep that healing "alive" within you?

Direct and simple questions can get complicated, often by the paralyzing effect of sin in our lives. We can then get confused as to how to respond to such essential questions. Every time we walk into the church, we are being asked by Christ, "Do you want to be healed?" Responding with a resounding "yes!" would signify the faith, hope, and love that are within us by the grace of God.

The Fourth Monday of May
Originally Written: May 2014

Mid-Pentecost: "Glistening with Splendor"

This week finds us at the exact midpoint of the sacred fifty-day period between the Feasts of Pascha and Pentecost. On Wednesday of this week, the twenty-fifth day of Pentecost and fourth Wednesday after Pascha is called, simply, Midfeast or Mid-Pentecost. Pentecost (from the Greek *pentecosti*) is, of course, the name of the great feast on the fiftieth day after Pascha, but the term is also used to cover the entire fifty-day period linking the two feasts, thus expressing their profound inner unity. Our emphasis on the greatness of Pascha – the "feast of feasts" – may at times come at the expense of Pentecost, but in an essential manner Pascha is dependent upon Pentecost for its ultimate fulfillment. As Professor Veselin Kesich wrote, "Because of Pentecost, the resurrection of Christ is a present reality, not just an event that belongs to the past." Kallistos Ware states that,

> we do not say merely, "Christ rose," but "Christ is risen" – He lives now, for me and in me. This immediacy and personal directness in our relationship with Jesus is precisely the work of the Spirit. Any transformation of human life is testimony to the resurrection of Christ and the descent of the Spirit on the day of Pentecost. God constantly creates new things and glorifies Himself in His saints, in order to make it known that the Word of God became flesh, experienced death on the cross, and was raised up that we might receive the Spirit.[*]

Be that as it may, there is a wonderful hymn from the Vespers of the Midfeast that reveals this profound inner connection:

---

[*] *The Orthodox Way* (Crestwood, NY: St Vladimir's Seminary Press, 1979), 125.

> The middle of the fifty days has come, beginning with the Savior's resurrection, and sealed by the Holy Pentecost. The first and the last glisten with splendor. We rejoice in the union of both feasts, as we draw near to the Lord's ascension – the sign of our coming glorification.

Pascha and Pentecost "glisten with splendor" – what a wonderful expression! Yet, this very phrase, indicative of the festal life of the Church, may also sound embarrassingly archaic to our ears today. This is not exactly an everyday expression, even when we encounter something above the ordinary. However, that could also say more about ourselves than the Church's less-than-contemporary vocabulary. Perhaps the drab conformity of our environment; the de-sacralized nature of the world around us, together with its prosaic concerns and uninspiring goals; and even the reduction of religion to morality and vague "values," make us more than a little cynical about the mere prospect of anything "glistening with splendor." How can Pascha and Pentecost "glisten with splendor" if Pascha quickly becomes a forgotten experience of the past, and if the upcoming feasts of Ascension and Pentecost fail to fill us with the least bit of expectation or anticipation?

The Lord is risen, and we await the coming of the Comforter, the "Spirit of truth." These are two awesome claims! The Apostle Paul exhorts us: "Set your minds on the things that are above, not on things that are on earth" (Col 3.2). This is a great challenge, for experience teaches us that "the things that are on earth" can be very compelling, immediate, and deeply attractive, while "the things that are above" can seem abstract and distant; or that they are reserved for the end of our life as we know it "on earth." The Apostle Paul is exhorting us to a radical reorientation of our approach to life – what we may call our "vision of life" – and again, this is difficult, even for believing Christians. Yet, I would like to believe that with our minds lifted and our hearts turned inward to where God is, not only will the feasts themselves "glisten with splendor," but so will our souls. Then, what the world believes to be unattainable, will be precisely the experience that makes us "not of the world." May the days to come somehow, by the grace of God, "glisten with splendor!" As it is written,

> The abundant outpouring of divine gifts is drawing near. The chosen day of the Spirit is halfway come. The faithful promise to the disciples after the death, burial and resurrection of Christ heralds the coming of the Comforter! (Vespers of the Midfeast)

The Fifth Monday of May
Originally Written: May 2014

From Where Do We Draw Our Water?

In my humble opinion, the conversation between Jesus and the Samaritan woman (Jn 4.5–42) may be the most profound and amazing dialog ever recorded in human history. There are, of course, the incredible Platonic dialogs concerning the irrepressible Socrates and his quest for moral and ethical truth. With Jesus, however, someone greater than Socrates is present. We were blessed yet again yesterday – the Sunday of the Samaritan Woman – to hear this passage during the Liturgy. The incomparable quality of this discourse stems not only from the content but also from the identity of the two protagonists. This will be discussed more fully below. For the moment, we need to realize that this great dialog has a carefully conceived and executed literary structure. That literary structure adds to the inherent drama, refined characterization, theological depth, and overall quality of this unique and unforgettable scene in St John's Gospel. This is an inspired text that can be read over and over yet still inspire the reader with its endless insights into the revelation that comes in and through Jesus Christ, "the Savior of the world" (v. 42).

Jesus sat down by the well because He was "wearied" from His journey. This fatigue reveals the true humanity of Jesus. Having "become flesh," He was subject to the "blameless passions," those weaknesses of the flesh that are inherent to our human nature within the conditions of this fallen world. That would include hunger, thirst, fear, suffering, and death. Jesus is not a divine figure roaming the world incognito under the illusory veil of human flesh. He does not merely *seem* to be human. The Word actually became flesh, therefore freely accepting the human frailty that we all experience. Refreshing himself at the well, Jesus was joined by a woman, a Samaritan, who came to draw water and take it back to her village. At this point, the dialog commences between the two and, since they are at the well, their conversation initially centers on the theme of water. As is typical in these dialogs recorded in St John's Gospel, a particular word or phrase carries a double meaning – earthly and spiritual, we could say. Jesus informs the woman that if she had asked for a gift from God, she would have received "living water." The woman, thinking in earthly or natural terms, would like to receive living water, i.e., water that is fresh and flowing, coming from a fountain or stream and not from a well or cistern. But Jesus, who has come to reveal heavenly things, elevates the conversation to a spiritual level. By "living water," He draws on Old Testament allusions that equate water with divine wisdom and revelation. And "living water" also becomes a clear reference to the Holy Spirit, a point that is made explicit a bit later in the Gospel: "He who believes in me, as the Scripture has said, 'Out of his heart shall flow rivers of living water.' Now this he said about the Spirit, which those who believe in him were to receive; for as yet the Spirit had not been given, because Jesus was not yet glorified" (Jn 7.38–39).

The Samaritan woman responds with a certain confusion. She still cannot understand how Jesus can draw this "living water." (She is not even sure why Jesus would speak with her – a woman of Samaria – "for Jews had no dealings with Samaritans" [Jn 4.9]). Disregarding her objections, Jesus elaborates and elevates His meaning, culminating in a magnificent definition of baptism of water and of Spirit: "Every one who drinks of this water will thirst again, but whoever drinks of the water that I shall give him will never thirst; the water that I shall give him will become in him a spring of water welling up to eternal life" (4.13–14).

At this point, the words of Jesus are beginning to penetrate the mind and heart of the Samaritan woman. Something about

Jesus and about what He is saying is attracting her to His enigmatic words. (As the narrative progresses, she ultimately comes to believe that Jesus is the Messiah [Jn 4.29, 39].) Her response captures her slow movement from the earthly level to the beginning of her elevation to the spiritual level, for her "request" vocalizes a "thirst" that is progressing beyond the merely natural level: "The woman said to him, 'Sir, give me this water, that I may not thirst, nor come here to draw'" (4.15).

As articulately as St John the Evangelist captures the unique character of the Samaritan woman, she also represents the thirst of humanity, and the endless existential quest to satisfy that thirst. Like her, we all seek after the "well" – *any* well – from which to draw some "water" that will sustain our search and quench our longing for something more in life. The choices are endless. The wells are attractively presented. In our restlessness and spiritual confusion, we go from well to well, drinking this or that water, but always ending up with an unquenchable thirst. As much as our secularism and pop-culture frenzy has seemingly stifled the spiritual thirst that was more apparent in the past, the human spirit still thirsts for the Holy Spirit of God. That is why the choices and the frenzied pursuits of the world are multiplying to a dizzying degree. If we try hard enough, perhaps we can cover up that basic human need for the divine. Perhaps we can make the thirst go away by drinking endlessly from a variety of wells. Or, perhaps there is nothing "out there" to satisfy our thirst. Perhaps the thirst is only an illusion.

Even though we are believing and practicing Orthodox Christians, do we periodically succumb to the temptation of such beliefs and patterns? Do we try and quench our own thirst at "wells" other than the well of the Gospel and the Eucharist? Do we believe that if we travel enough, spend enough, and accumulate enough, we can fool ourselves into thinking that we will quench our thirst? Why drink from the living water of the Gospels, when one can drink the stimulating water of a soap opera, novel, or splashy magazine? Why drink from the cup of the Bridegroom of the Church when one can dream of luxuriating in the whirlpools of the latest "Bachelorette" or "Bachelor" television series? Why observe a fast of the Church when we can eat and drink to our heart's content? Why drink from the difficult teaching of Jesus in the Sermon on the Mount when we can easily quench our thirst with the latest self-help book or the guidance of a financial guru? Of course, we will continue to go to church and fulfill our "religious obligations," but the Church may only provide a "reservoir" of water kept for emergency situations. The real "fun" begins after and outside of Church. These are the types of temptations that we must always be vigilant toward. Yet, this leaves us with the question: *from where do we draw our "water"?*

When the Samaritan woman eventually left the well to return to her village and tell her fellow villagers about Jesus, she left behind the water jar that she had brought with her to the well. This small detail did not escape the vigilant eye of the evangelist. She no longer thirsted for the water from the well, but was now intent upon the living water that came through the presence and teaching of Jesus. When we worship the Father, we receive the "living water" of "Spirit and truth." This is an inexhaustible font of "water" that quenches our thirst for the meaning of life. The Spirit guides us in a life that is lived within the light of God's design for the world. It is the gift of God that we can ask Jesus for, and He will give it to us as He promised the woman of Samaria.

The First Monday of June
Originally Written: June 2014

Too Busy NOT to Pray

While looking through a catalog from a Christian publishing company, I recently came across a rather intriguing advertisement for a book called *Too Busy Not to Pray*.[*] I say intriguing because the title touches on a theme I think about often and have raised with others before. Read that title again carefully, because it does not say *Too Busy to Pray*, but precisely *Too Busy* Not *to Pray*. Either title could serve as an invitation to a book that presumably addresses the contemporary Christian's struggle to maintain a regular prayer life amid his or her busy schedule. However, the title as it stands captures the *urgency* of the issue much more effectively. I would express that urgency in the following manner: If we are indeed "too busy," then the only way that we can prevent our lives from spinning out of control – or of losing a God-directed orientation or reducing prayer to moments of danger and stress – is for the "busy person" to be ever-vigilant about praying with regularity to guard against such spiritual catastrophes.

We always need to pray with regularity – "pray without ceasing" (1 Thess 5.17). But it strikes me that the busier we are, the more urgent it becomes for us to pray. In other words, the busy person cannot afford not to pray. Busy people indeed need the nourishment of prayer. Otherwise, the spiritual dangers are immense. The "business" of our lives make us too busy to do what? We are certainly not "too busy" to socialize, to seek entertainment, pleasure, and diversion – all necessary to one degree or another because of the pressures of work and other responsibilities. And these diversions are layered onto lives that are already feeling the strain of

---

[*] Bill Hybels, *Too Busy Not to Pray* (Downers Grove: InterVarsity Press, 2008).

"multi-tasking" the endless activities that keep our children educated, developing, healthily preoccupied, etc. (A social commentator recently wrote that mothers have been reduced to the roles of domestic caretakers and chauffeurs. And it is difficult to deny that fathers have also suffered a certain diminution in their roles.) Most people construct their schedules carefully so that these extra social and diversionary activities are not terribly neglected. We can cast this under the rubrics of "leisure" or "recreational time." (This all gets a bit sloppy when we go further and speak of "vegging out.") It is the careful, calculated, and natural integration of such activities into our lives that leaves us with the overwhelming certainty that we are too busy, which in turn leaves us too tired.

And at that point, we just may be. The question then arises again, now with a certain persistence: too busy to do (or not do) what? To pray, to read the Scriptures, to assist a needy neighbor, to visit someone who really needs a visit, or even to call someone we know who is lonely? We are "too busy" to integrate the life of the Church into our lives beyond Sunday mornings. We are "too busy" for Vespers, Bible studies, feast days, etc. Perhaps, finally, we are too busy for God. How often do we postpone our relationship with God until we have more time? "If only my life would slow down a bit, then I could turn my attention to God, beyond the perfunctory rushed prayer of my busy, daily life – if I even get to it."

Is this dilemma unavoidable and irresolvable? Every Christian who does face – or *face up to* – this dilemma must search his or her heart and ask, "how is it that I am 'too busy' to pray?" Whatever honest answers we come up with, I am convinced that we, indeed, are *too busy* not *to pray*.

The Second Monday of June
Originally Written: June 2016

Forty-Nine Plus One:
Pentecost and the Life beyond Time

At the Vespers of Pentecost celebrated on Pentecost Sunday, we implore the risen Lord, seated at the right hand of God the Father, to send the Holy Spirit upon us, as He did upon the apostles who "were all together in one place" (Acts 2.1). It is significant that Pentecost occurred exactly fifty days after the resurrection of Christ. In the ancient world, there was a deep symbolic – even sacred – character to the use of numbers, and this is reflected in the Scriptures. Fr Alexander Schmemann explains this "sacred numerology" as it relates to the Feast of Pentecost:

> Pentecost in Greek means 50, and in the sacred biblical symbolism of numbers, the number 50 symbolizes both the fullness of time and that which is beyond time: the Kingdom of God itself. It symbolizes the fullness of time by its first component – 49 – which is the fullness of seven (7 x 7): the number of time. And, it symbolizes that which is beyond time by its second component – 49 + 1 – this one being the new day, the "day without evening" of God's eternal Kingdom. With the descent of the Holy Spirit upon Christ's disciples, the time of salvation, the divine work of redemption has been completed, the fullness revealed, all gifts bestowed; it belongs to us now to "appropriate" these gifts, to be that which we have become in Christ: participants and citizens of His Kingdom.[*]

[*] "Pentecost: The Feast of the Church," in *The Vespers of Pentecost* (Syosset, NY: Department of Religious Education OCA, 1974), 1-2.

This reality takes us beyond time as experienced in this world, to that which is eschatological – the fullness of the kingdom of God which, while "not of this world," is yet experienced here and now within the grace-filled life of the Church.

The appropriation of the gifts of the Holy Spirit, referred to above by Fr Schmemann, implies the rejection of a way of life that is described as fleshly. In an extraordinary passage by the Apostle Paul in his Epistle to the Galatians, we encounter the contrast between the "works of the flesh" and the "fruit of the Spirit" (Gal 5.16–24). St Paul emphasizes this contrast at the beginning of this passage:

> But I say to you, walk by the Spirit, and do not gratify the desires of the flesh. For the desires of the flesh are against the Spirit, and the desires of the Spirit are against the flesh; for these are opposed to each other, to prevent you from doing what you would. But if you are led by the Spirit you are not under the law. (Gal 5.16–17)

It is essential to recognize that by "flesh," the Apostle Paul does not refer to our bodies or physical existence as a whole. That would imply a dualism, an artificial and non-Scriptural conflict between the spiritual and the material. Instead, the Apostle Paul is referring to the human person in rebellion against God, a state of being that results in a self-centered way of life that further perverts both body and soul. As this passage continues, one can clearly discern the comprehensive nature of the "flesh" as encompassing both the mind and body, directing them to sinful activities or attitudes: "Now the works of the flesh are plain: immorality, impurity, licentiousness, idolatry, sorcery, enmity, strife, jealousy, anger, selfishness, dissension, party spirit, envy, drunkenness, carousing, and the like" (Gal 5.19–21).

My intention is not to be discouraging, but if anything here sounds self-descriptive or reminiscent of one's most recent confession, then one is still contending with the "works of the flesh."

According to the apostle, the long-term prospects for such a way of life are not very promising, if not altogether bleak: "I warn you, as I warned you before, that those who do such things shall not inherit the kingdom of God" (Gal 5.21).

However, the "good news" is that there exists another way of life, one that is spiritual but expressed through bodily existence in the rhythms of our daily life: "But the fruit of the Spirit is love, joy, peace, patience, kindness, goodness, faithfulness, gentleness, self-control; against such there is no law" (Gal 5.22–23). In this catalog of the fruits of the Spirit, there is no mention of grand miracles, visions, ecstatic, or mystical experiences. Instead, St Paul calls upon simple, human virtues, but with the implication that they are heightened – or deepened – by the Holy Spirit in a way that manifests a new manner of living, one he calls elsewhere a "new creation" (2 Cor 5.17). This newness of life in the Holy Spirit distinguished the early Christians from their environment and is meant to distinguish Christians to this day. The failure to live by the "fruit of the Spirit" is essentially a failure of our Christian vocation. St Paul implies as much when he writes with confidence: "And those who belong to Christ Jesus have crucified the flesh with its passions and desires" (Gal 5.24).

A final exhortation elucidates the behavioral consequences of this newness of life made possible by the Holy Spirit: "If we live by the Spirit, let us also walk by the Spirit. Let us have no self-conceit, no provoking of one another, no envy of one another" (Gal 5.25). As members of the original pentecostal Church, Orthodox Christians have every opportunity to both "live by the Spirit" and "walk by the Spirit."

The Third Monday of June
Originally Written: May 2010

The Day of the Holy Spirit

The aim of the Christian life is to return to that perfect grace of the most holy and life-giving Spirit, which was originally conferred upon us through divine baptism.

– St Ignatios Xanthopoulos and St Kallistos

Although the Feast of Pentecost reveals the trinitarian nature of God, it is on this "last and great day of Pentecost" that we concentrate on the Holy Spirit. This is clear from the prescribed readings for the Sunday of Pentecost: Acts 2.1–11, which describes the descent of the Holy Spirit on the Day of Pentecost; and John 7.37–52, 8.12, which speaks of the giving of the Holy Spirit by the glorified Christ. As Orthodox Christians, we do not reduce the Holy Spirit to a kind of indefinite divine power or energy but instead proclaim that the Holy Spirit is God, the "third Person" of the "holy, consubstantial, life-creating, and undivided Trinity."

We further believe that the Holy Spirit "proceeds from the Father" (Jn 15.26), and "with the Father and the Son together is worshiped and glorified" (*Nicene Creed*). As one of the many beautiful hymns of the Vespers of Pentecost expresses:

> The Holy Spirit was, is, and ever shall be
> Without beginning, without end,
> Forever united and numbered with the Father
> and the Son.

The Holy Spirit, present within the dispensation of the Old Testament and more openly within the earthly ministry of Christ, descends into the world in a unique (but decisive and final) way on the great day of Pentecost, fifty days after the Savior's resurrection.

The coming of the Holy Spirit gave birth to the New Testament Church and the Holy Spirit abides in the Church as the life-giving power of renewal, rebirth, and regeneration. The Church would grow old and die (as do empires, nations, cultures, and secular institutions) because of our many human and historical sins, if not for this presence of the Holy Spirit, making the Church ever-young and cleansing us all "from every impurity" as the personal source of sanctification.

We come to the Father through the Son and in the power of the Holy Spirit. Or, as St Gregory of Nyssa elaborates:

> One does not think of the Father without the Son and one does not conceive of the Son without the Holy Spirit. For it is impossible to attain to the Father except by being raised by the Son, and it is impossible to call Jesus Lord save in the Holy Spirit.

All authentic life in the Church is life lived in the Holy Trinity, and on the day of Pentecost the coming of the Holy Spirit is the final revelation of precisely this greatest of mysteries – that the one God is "tri-hypostatic" (meaning "tri-personal"), existing as the Father, the Son, and the Holy Spirit. As this quotation from St Thalassios the Libyan reveals, the Church fathers understand the Trinity as a paradox:

> The single divinity of the Trinity is undivided and the three Persons of the one divinity are unconfused. We confess Unity in Trinity and Trinity in Unity, divided yet without division and united yet with distinctions.

While the Sunday of Pentecost is the Feast of the Holy Trinity, Pentecost Monday is the day of the Holy Spirit. St Basil the Great enumerates the divine attributes of the Holy Spirit:

> From this Source comes foreknowledge of the future, the understanding of mysteries, the apprehension of things hidden, the partaking of spiritual gifts, the heavenly citizenship, a place in the choir of angels, unending joy, the power to abide in God, to become like God, and, highest of all ends to which we can aspire, to become divine.
> (*On the Holy Spirit* 9.23)

This can strike us as abstract, but theology reveals to us the foundation and the vision on which and in which we order our spiritual lives. The dogma of the Trinity must impact our lives. As Orthodox Christians, we must know the God that we worship, for we do not worship an "unknown God" (Acts 17.22–34). We are not Deists or Unitarians, neither are we monotheists in the same manner as Jews and Muslims; we are trinitarian monotheists. "We have seen the true Light!" It does not help to simply say, "We all believe in the same God." If we have been taught, and then teach our own children, to make the sign of the cross "in the name of the Father, and of the Son, and of the Holy Spirit," then we need to understand what we are proclaiming by this simple but profound gesture. As we pray, we need also to study. No Orthodox Christian should be intimidated by the dogma of the Holy Trinity, protesting ignorance or a false humility as a cover up for intellectual or spiritual laziness. There is clarity to be found in truth – a profound mystery is not an obscure riddle. If your neighbor asks you what you mean by the Holy Trinity, then you must be prepared to say something simple and to the point – and accurate. The saints have suffered and died for their belief in the Holy Trinity. We honor them by our own commitment to receive this "true faith" in a spirit of worship, prayer, humility, and the burning desire to illuminate our minds and hearts with the triune presence of God.

The beginning of this process of discerning the presence of God in our lives and in trying to live out that presence is to be found in the sacraments of baptism and chrismation. Every person baptized and chrismated into the life of the Orthodox Church has participated in his or her own personal Pascha and Pentecost. To be baptized is to die and rise in Christ; to be chrismated is to receive "the seal of the gift of the Holy Spirit." We are alive in Christ, sealed and filled with the Holy Spirit, having partaken of new life and the power with which and in which we are enabled to continue in that life.

Without Christ, we "can do nothing" (Jn 15.5), and without the Holy Spirit – poured out upon us by the risen, ascended and glorified Christ at Pentecost – we cannot say that "Jesus is Lord" (1 Cor 12.3).

As St Seraphim of Sarov put it: "The true goal of our Christian life consists in the acquisition of the Spirit of God." Yet I cannot help but wonder whether – or to what extent – we are troubled if we squander the great grace of baptism that we received when we were buried with Christ in the baptismal font, which represents both a tomb (dying to sin) and a womb (rebirth). It seems as if we can be insensitive to the withdrawal of the Spirit's presence from our minds and hearts through sheer inattention and lack of vigilance.

The saints would weep for their sins – in fact, this is called "the gift of tears," the means of restoring that very baptismal grace forfeited by sin – while we shrug off our own sins as normal and practically inevitable considering the conditions and circumstances of life. If we are "like other people" in conformity with a basic set of moral principles, and thus maintaining a good image in the eyes of others, then we are usually perfectly content with our own sinfulness. In this way, we domesticate and normalize sin by rendering it innocuous and easy to live with. We redefine sin into something that hardly resembles what we find in the Scriptures, that tragic "missing of the mark," a baneful reality from which we needed to be saved by the death of our Savior.

But how we may weep and gnash our teeth when we lose money, property, status, or simply "things"; how we mourn the loss of even a trinket if we have invested it with sentimental value. These types of losses attract our concern, muting out the "voice" of the Spirit so that it draws only a lukewarm sigh from our conscience.

This is an unfortunate reversal of values. Losing the "seal of the Gift of the Holy Spirit" is tantamount to losing our "heavenly treasure," while losing our earthly treasures is only to lose what "moth and rust consume" despite our heroic efforts to escape that process. This is a paradox: when, by the grace of God, our spiritual lives have matured in such a way that we truly mourn (and even weep!) over our sins which strip us of the presence of the "comforter and spirit of truth," then through genuine repentance, the Holy Spirit will "come and abide in us" to "warm our hearts with perfect love," according to the words of St Seraphim of Sarov.

> *The Lord gave us the Holy Spirit, and the person in whom the Holy Spirit lives feels that he has paradise within.*
> (St Silouan of Mt Athos)

The Fourth Monday of June
Originally Written: June 2015

Finding Our "Self" in the Other:
Reflections on National Selfie Day

As I write this, it is evidently National Selfie Day (June 21). I find this unofficial holiday a bit absurd, but perhaps indicative of our society's pulse. Nonetheless, it provides a moment to reflect as Orthodox Christians not only on the phenomenon of the selfie, but also by extension the idea of the self. The selfie, I believe, is something of an unintended caricature of the search for the self — not really the dark side of the self, but its superficial side.

From therapists to talk-show hosts and even "spiritual teachers," we are enjoined to "discover," "get in touch with," or "enhance" our "self." We now hear of popular personalities "reinventing" themselves as they "move on" to a new phase of life and experience. And perhaps the most indulgent of this self-expression is the phenomenon of the selfie. In all this, there seems to be an implicit understanding of just what this mysterious "self" actually consists of, since we refer to it so often and so readily.

But is there common ground as to what we mean by this term? If we were to depend on more-or-less contemporary psychology or the behavioral sciences, we might believe that the self is our "personal identity" — what constitutes each one of us as a unique human being. After all, we distinguish each other by referring to "myself," "yourself," "himself/herself," and so on, thus concentrating on our individuality. On the other hand, to have a self could also refer to our consciousness and ability to reflect upon our existence — I know that I am alive and that one day I will die, therefore I have the capacity for "self-awareness." Or is the self simply synonymous with the "I" or "ego"?

Buddhism rejects the very idea of the self, calling it an illusion created by our constant desiring. Perhaps Buddhists are less self-absorbed than we are. Still, we do not agree with them on this crucial issue. As Christians, we accept the self as integral to being human. However, as noted above, our contemporary preoccupation with the self borders on the obsessive and idolatrous. Life is presented as a long and exciting journey of self-discovery. However, in reality is this not the ultimate ego trip, an endless journey toward "self-delusion"? Frankly, a great deal of today's talk about the self sounds terribly superficial. It is a far cry from the Delphic oracle's ancient maxim, taken up by later philosophers: "Know thyself!"

Whenever theology ceases to be "God-centered" (and the word God – *Theos* – is in the word theology) and is instead reduced to a sophisticated anthropology (reality as human-centered), we should be alert to the tendency toward self-focus. This is why many New Testament scholars are critical of the attempt to bring some of the non-canonical Gospels into prominence. These heretical and gnostic "Gospels" are essentially about discovering the god within. The "spirituality" they advocate is really about self-realization, if not self-deification. Even the depth psychologist David Benner has succinctly written: "When the spiritual journey is my own self-improvement project, the major product will be an ego that is even more in control than before the journey began."[*]

According to our spiritual tradition, we are not ourselves because we are fallen and sinful. This is biblical. A recognition of that fact may just serve as a good beginning to discover our "true self." And this is why Evagrius of Pontus, a desert ascetic, could write: "The beginning of salvation is self-condemnation." (You will certainly not find a book in the self-help section of the bookstore with such a title!)

[*] David G. Benner, *Spirituality and the Awakening of the Self: The Sacred Journey of Transformation* (Grand Rapids, MI: Brazos Press, 2012), 158.

Evagrius' exhortation is not a call to unhealthy self-hatred but rather encourages us to recognize our sin and the need to repent and be freed from the useless refuge of self-justification. Whatever the self may be in relation to some of the suggestions I offered, the real question becomes: what is the foundation or ground of the self? What guarantees its stability and continuity? What prevents the self from being one more fleeting and ephemeral reality, so much "dust in the wind" that goes the way of our bodies? If anything is that source, it must be God. Either the self is rooted and secured in God, or it is grounded in nothing. We are either "God-sourced" or "nothing-sourced." If the latter, then the self is unstable and ever on the brink of disappearing into the void.

Perhaps all the clamorous cries of "self-affirmation" we hear today are instinctive reactions or even rebellions against this inherent nihilism. A godless quest of self-discovery leads to a dead-end encounter with our own nothingness. Do atheistic therapists and secular counselors remind their clients of that cold fact? That last statement needs to be qualified to avoid any misunderstanding as to my intended meaning. Undoubtedly, there exist many wonderful "self-help" groups and therapies that have been very effective in helping people overcome a wide range of aberrant behavioral problems, especially those plagued by addictions. Perhaps the most well-known is Alcoholics Anonymous, a therapy grounded in the Gospel that has rescued countless men and women from alcoholism. To this day, many people have recourse to such helpful societies in combating their destructive behavior, and thus saving themselves from seemingly hopeless situations.

At the same time, a healthy "self-reliance" is cultivated and restored in persons who need such a change. Many of these self-help groups acknowledge the existence of God and thus apply their respective therapies within a theistic context. This adds a dimension of humility to the whole process. However, it is not quite this phenomenon that I have been referring to throughout this meditation, but rather the empty promises, and even pseudo-theologies, that lead to an unwholesome fixation with the self. Something must give in contemporary self-obsession that has generated an endless market for books, tapes, CDs, DVDs, seminars, programs, therapies, self-help gurus and the like that distances us from the teaching of our Lord: "If any man would come after me, let him deny himself" (Mk 8.34).

This is not a Buddhist-like call to "self-transcendence" in search of enlightenment. It is Christ's way of teaching us that to defensively, fearfully, or even idolatrously hold onto the self as some sort of autonomous entity will only culminate in the loss of our life. To deny such a self-centered way of existence for the sake of the Gospel is to "save" our lives.

"Life" and "self" are very closely equated in this crucial passage. Further, the word "life" is synonymous with the word "soul." Each of us is a living soul, formed by the creative power of God and having received the "breath of life" that sustains us and lifts us up beyond the merely biological level of existence.

Employing our theological language further, we should also equate self with the person. (The theological term is *hypostasis*.) Every living soul is a person – unique, unrepeatable, and beloved of God. As the three divine persons of the Holy Trinity are never self-isolated, self-absorbed, or self-centered, so we realize that that would be a false way of existing. A genuine person is always turned toward another person in a movement of love and communion, as are the three persons of the Trinity. This gives us great insight into the teaching, "You shall love your neighbor as yourself" (Mk 12.31).

"To be" is to be in communion, as one of our contemporary Orthodox theologians has explained. If we could pour our energy into discovering the "wholly other" – God, and the multiple others – the neighbor; then we would uncover our "true self" in the process. Our tradition tells us to find our "self" in the other — God and neighbor. Being a living soul and/or a person, then, describes a mode of being, a way of life, that is as far removed from the thinly-veiled narcissism that passes today as "self-realization," as the "East is from the West."

Orthodox Christianity affirms the self, but as dependent for its very existence upon the creative power of God and the redemptive grace of Christ. Each of us is created, sustained, and guided by God toward a destiny so glorious that it is essentially indescribable. It is this humble acknowledgement of dependence on God that becomes the foundation of that long process that will lead us from being "self-centered" to being "God-centered." Perhaps we can go so far as to say that we seek to be *saved* from our "self" to truly *be* ourselves in the embrace of God. Today's world seems oblivious of this promise.

The First Monday of July
Originally Written: July 2013

July: A Month-Long Spiritual Desert

Unless we find ourselves on an exciting vacation somewhere far from home, it seems that nothing can conceivably be more uneventful than a Monday morning in mid-July. Often the only "variety" is the weather. Will it rain or will the sun shine? Will the blistering heat continue, or will we feel some relief? At this point in the summer, we may have already been on vacation – which means there isn't much to look forward to – or we are awaiting an upcoming trip that at least fills us with some sense of anticipation and escape. This poses a further question: are those carefully planned vacations always as rewarding, relaxing, and renewing as expected? Whatever the case, the following passage from the Scriptures may inspire us to see beyond the tedium that leads to the forgetfulness of God: "Therefore lift your drooping hands and strengthen your weak knees, and make straight paths for your feet, so that what is lame may not be put out of joint but rather healed" (Heb 12.12–13).

Adding to our spiritual *ennui* is, admittedly, the fact that July is the most uneventful month of the year, liturgically speaking: no major fasts or feasts occur during this month. Basically, there is "only" the Liturgy on Sundays and the commemoration of a few well-known saints throughout the month. With vacationing parishioners, there can be a noticeable drop in church attendance. Certain signs of "spiritual laziness" may also set in (induced in part, perhaps, by the languid weather), leading to that condition of spiritual torpor our spiritual literature calls *acedia*. July, therefore, is something of a month-long stretch of desert, for we have celebrated the Feast of Sts Peter and Paul (June 29) and await the major Feasts of the Transfiguration and Dormition in August.

Of course, we never want to find ourselves saying that there is "only" the Liturgy on Sunday mornings. "Only" is a hopelessly inadequate word when applied to celebration of the Eucharist on the Lord's Day. It implies that our eucharistic service is ordinary or uneventful. Yet, every Liturgy essentially actualizes, or makes present, the paschal mystery of the death and resurrection of Christ, and our participation in that mystery. At every Liturgy, we proclaim and bless the presence and power of the kingdom of heaven. We praise and pray to the Holy Trinity together with the angels and the saints. We stand in direct communion with God and one another in the Liturgy. This means that every Liturgy is "eventful" in a manner that we can barely comprehend!

If, indeed, the summer proves to be something of a spiritual drought, we can only thank God for the weekly liturgical cycle that begins and culminates with the Divine Liturgy and allows us to renew our genuine humanity that has been created, redeemed, and transformed "in Christ." To speak of our life "in Christ" on the communal level, we believe that every Liturgy anticipates the messianic banquet when "many will come from east and west and sit at table with Abraham, Isaac, and Jacob in the kingdom of heaven" (Mt 8.11). The heavenly manna, i.e., the "Bread from heaven" that we receive by the grace of God, strengthens us in the somewhat outward and inward "desert-like" conditions of the world around (or within) us.

On a more interior level, we may one day discover that we need not travel far away geographically to embark upon a life-transforming journey. In the Prologue to his book *The Orthodox Way*, Metropolitan Kallistos Ware relates the following anecdote:

> One of the best known of the Desert Fathers of fourth-century Egypt, St Sarapion the Sidonite, travelled once on pilgrimage to Rome. Here he was told of a celebrated recluse, a woman who lived always in one small room, never going out. Sceptical about her way of life – for he was

himself a great wanderer – Sarapion called on her and asked: "Why are you sitting here?" To this she replied: "I am not sitting, I am on a journey."*

Admittedly, this will not work well with the children. But at one point in our lives, we need desperately to make that discovery of our interior depths wherein we find a point of stillness that quells the excessive restlessness that endlessly pushes us "outward" rather than "inward." Elsewhere in the same book, Metropolitan Kallistos puts it this way: "We are on a journey through the inward space of the heart, a journey not measured by the hours of our watch or the days of the calendar, for it is a journey out of time into eternity."**

"Vacations" are one thing, and "journeys" (or pilgrimages) another. The packaging and planning of the former make them much more predictable than the limitless possibilities of the latter. As we plan our outward vacations by plane or car, we need to make provisions for the interior journeys into the greater space of our hearts through faith, hope, and love, as well as through the practices of prayer and fasting, to remain attentive to the voice of God that imbues our lives with direction and meaning.

We pray that God will bless us as we embark on both forms of travel.

---

* Bishop Kallistos Ware, *The Orthodox Way* (Crestwood, NY: St Vladimir's Seminary Press, 1979), 7.
** Ibid.

The Second Monday of July
Originally Written: August 2009

Bored by Sin

Perhaps some will recall the film *Groundhog Day* that was released in 1991. If not quite a cult classic (it was too mainstream for that), it was immensely popular and subject to an endless flow of commentary and interpretation. The lead role seemed to be a perfect fit for Bill Murray's deadpan and ironic sense of humor. Having enjoyed the film myself, and having viewed it a few times in the years since, I suggested *Groundhog Day* for our latest "Feature Film Festival" that was organized with our parish high school students. Yesterday evening found us watching the film together, and I believe it was thoroughly enjoyed by all – there was certainly a great deal of laughter!

Yet, the purpose of watching films together, beyond the social significance of gathering as a group, is to find those films that are morally and ethically probing, in addition to their "entertainment value." Movies and movie-going dominate our popular culture, so trying to deepen that experience a bit strikes me as a sound idea. When selecting movies to view in parish gatherings, we try and choose films that will make everyone think and provide a substantive basis for a post-film discussion. So why choose a film such as *Groundhog Day*, a film often described as "zany" and "wacky"? There is no doubt that it plays as an entertaining romantic comedy. However, there are also layers of meaning underneath that rather well-worn and rather predictable genre. How many people know that at least for a few years after its release, *Groundhog Day* was subject to a great deal of philosophical and even theological commentary and interpretation? I recall reading numerous insightful reviews of this film in some rather "high-brow" journals. What makes that even more intriguing is that the director, Harold Ramis, claims that the philosophical implications so many thinkers encountered in *Groundhog Day* went beyond his intention in making the film. The creative process can be mysterious.

The film is essentially a romantic comedy with a real twist. It charts the life of a cynical and ambitious Pittsburgh weatherman, Phil Connors (played perfectly by Bill Murray). His self-absorption and unapologetic egotism are of gargantuan proportions; his charm is manipulative and self-serving. As the center of the universe, apparently everyone and everything around him is meant to satisfy his needs and desires. Indeed, he admits later in the film that he is a "real jerk." Phil the weatherman is sent to Punxsutawney, PA to cover the Groundhog Day festivities there. In his mind, it promises to be a boring excursion into small-town existence. At one point, he contemptuously calls the local population "hicks." He is accompanied by his TV station's producer, Rita, and camera operator, Larry. It is obvious Phil does not want to be there, and can't leave soon enough once his responsibilities are fulfilled. However, a blizzard he failed to predict sends him back to the small town for at least one more night. When confronted with the storm, he angrily shouts back to the highway patrol man: "I make the weather!" But even he is forced to succumb to the power of nature – back to town he goes.

Phil wakes up the "next day" only to discover that it is February 2 and Groundhog Day all over again – exactly, down to every detail. He awakens in the same bed-and-breakfast room at the same time to the sounds of the same old pop song blaring on the radio. As he moves through the halls and downstairs to breakfast, he has the same inane encounters with the same fellow guests. On the street, he witnesses the identical mundane activities being performed by the same people as the day(s) before – *ad nauseum*. He is trapped in an inexplicable temporal loop that forces him to relive the same day over and over again, apparently without end – into eternity itself. It is the myth of the eternal return, but lived out daily in small-town Punxsutawney! In short, it is a living nightmare.

The film wisely makes not even the slightest attempt at explaining this new reality. How could it? It simply *is*, and Phil is helplessly caught in it alone – no one else is aware of his temporal predicament. They remain as static and unchanging as the surrounding environment. Bewildered and frightened, Phil begins to make "adjustments" to his new situation. His selfish gene kicks into action. He soon realizes that his newly-achieved immortality means his actions have no future consequences, because there no longer exists a "tomorrow" in any meaningful or cumulative sense of the word. There is no one or nothing to answer to. As it plays out in the film, it is something of a lighthearted version of Dostoevsky's aphorism, "if there is no God, then everything is permissible." Phil can now break any conceivable law – civic, social, moral, divine – with total impunity. He can now unleash his hidden passions with no restraint or anticipatory anxiety. He can "eat, drink, and be merry" without the slightest cost to his well-being – or so it seems to him. The film exploits all of this to wonderful comic effect, and it is hard to dislike Phil in the process, "jerk" that he is. But perhaps our sympathy with Phil is grounded in the reality that he is living out some of our own uninspired fantasies. What would you do if you won a billion-dollar lottery? What would you do if there were no consequences to your actions?

One of the great insights of our spiritual tradition is that sin – beyond its moral, ethical, and spiritually corrupting effect – is ultimately boring. Besides immediate satisfaction, it remains a distortion of true life, and instead of yielding an enhanced sense of life – or "living life" as Dostoevsky would call it – sin devolves into an empty caricature of life. It is the negation of life. That is why spiritual death precedes biological death. Repetition is not a relief, but an increase of this intolerable boredom. The passions are insatiable. Sin is thus an existential vacuum that is suffocating in its long-term effects. Unconsciously, or perhaps intuitively, Phil begins to realize this after endless bouts of "wine, women, and song." Daily dissipation has worn him out. He embodies the biblical "vanity of vanities." His moral universe is unaware of a "higher reality," so he looks elsewhere for relief.

Although consistently maintaining its comic touch, the film now steers us in a darker direction. Attaining a sort of pseudo-omniscience by being able to predict the daily events around him, and realizing that he cannot die, Phil begins to fancy himself a "god." Not "the God" as he admits, but a "god" nevertheless. There is nothing new left to experience so he turns to suicide. Life is boring, so he will now try death! Phil now explores the many "creative" ways in which a person can commit suicide – from driving trucks over steep cliffs, swan-diving off tall buildings, or electrocuting himself in the bathtub. This can be interpreted as a grisly escape from the prison-like nature of repetitive, isolated existence; or the thoroughly desperate attempt to discover some more "kicks" in his morally meandering and meaningless existence.

But what "kicks in" at this point of the film is the slow transformation of Phil after he has bottomed out in the manner described above. The film has a "moral" that is not merely sentimental or banal, despite the genre and intent of this film. Remembering that this is a romantic comedy, the question becomes: will the guy – or how will the guy – get the girl in the end? Phil has resorted to endless subterfuge to seduce Rita, the producer. Try as he might, this is the one thing he could not succeed at, regardless of his great advantage of knowing her "inside out" after living an endless amount of days with her, each one ending with a well-deserved slap in the face as Phil's real intentions become obvious. Rita is quite attractive, but more importantly, she is a genuinely good person with a pure heart and honest intentions. Phil does not understand this within his warped moral sensitivity.

Yet, something happens within Phil and he begins to radically change by no longer living for himself alone. He somehow breaks through his narcissistic and solipsistic one-person universe. (There is a key scene involving a death in which he realizes that he is not actually a "god.") He discovers the "other," and this discovery is transformative. He begins to live altruistically. In fact, the film can be seen on one level as the transformation of Phil Connors from a self-identified jerk into a genuine human being. And this proves to be the way into the heart of Rita. Genuine virtue, as the great saints both taught and realized in their lives, is never boring if it does not lapse into formalism or moralism. It bears fruit a hundredfold when practiced with patience and the love of the "other" primarily in mind. It is the means of ascending the ladder of divine ascent, as St John Climacus demonstrated. Virtue is endlessly creative, since it extends and expands our humanity beyond the limits of the self. As Phil discovers, it is also the means of breaking through the meaningless "eternal return" that has taken him down into the inferno and back. But perhaps that is something that you may want to see for yourself.

Groundhog Day remains consistent from start to finish. The ending is satisfying and not simply anticlimactic. The screenplay is clever, sharp, and humorous, and regardless of its intentions – or lack thereof – it raises many profound issues that can be explored and expanded upon. I may have given away too much in my commentary, but I would still recommend it if you haven't seen it before. When we think of such topics as sin, repentance, and virtue, the film lends itself to a "Christian interpretation" that is not unduly forced, but rather flows naturally and instinctively from the predicament as conceived and presented. Such discoveries can be rewarding. All in all, a worthwhile film from a variety of perspectives.

The Third Monday of July
Originally Written: January 2008

Blessed Dissatisfaction

My soul thirsts for God, for the living God. (Ps 42.2)

Can't get no satisfaction. – The Rolling Stones

The driving guitar riff and raspy-voiced lyrics of the Rolling Stones classic "Can't Get no Satisfaction" articulate the disaffection of the lonely and alienated urbanite who, try as he might, just cannot manage to quench the material and sexual longings droned into his mind on the radio and TV. The song – regardless of the original actual intentions with which it was written – managed to say something enduring about the human condition. (Personally, I am inclined to believe that the members of the Rolling Stones did not derive a great amount of "satisfaction" from their enormous fame and fortune. Money and media exposure may, after all, just not be the solution.) Be that as it may, a rather odd connection came to me between this song and a verse from The Akathist of Thanksgiving: "Glory to You, Who have inspired in us dissatisfaction with earthly things" (*Ikos* 6). Both the Stones' song and the Orthodox hymn speak of dissatisfaction. However, by "earthly things," the author of this remarkable hymn, does not mean the natural world in which God has placed us. The refrain of *Ikos* 3 makes that abundantly clear:

> Glory to You, Who brought out of the earth's
> darkness diversity of color, taste and fragrance,
> Glory to You, for the warmth and
> caress of all nature,
> Glory to You, for surrounding us with
> thousands of Your creatures,

> Glory to You, for the depth of Your
> wisdom reflected in the whole world.

To the purified eyes of faith, the world around us can be a "festival of life… foreshadowing eternal life" (*Ikos* 2). The "earthly" can lead us toward the "heavenly."

"Earthly things" in the context of this akathist and the Orthodox worldview expressed in it, refer to the very things the Rolling Stones song laments as being lacking: material and sexual satisfaction seen as ends in themselves. Yet whereas their song expresses the frustration and resentment of being unable to fulfill such desires, the akathist glorifies God for the blessing of discontentment. In the light of the insight found in the words of this hymn, we can thus speak of a "blessed dissatisfaction." The Apostle Paul spoke of a closely-related "godly grief" (2 Cor 7.9–11). (Nevertheless, the Rolling Stones and the Orthodox Church part company at this point.)

This may prove to be quite a challenge to our way of approaching dissatisfaction. Our usual instinct is to flee from dissatisfaction as though from the plague. To be discontented implies unhappiness, together with a sense of deprivation and failure, the feeling that we are losing in the harsh game of life. Why should we tolerate the condition of dissatisfaction when there are limitless means of achieving "satisfaction" at our disposal? To escape from a gnawing sense of dissatisfaction, don't people resort to alcohol, drugs, and sex as desperate forms of relief? Or unrestrained and massive consumer spending? And we should not exclude "religion" as one of those means of escape. If those means fail, therapy, and medication offer more aggressive ways to relieve us of this unendurable feeling.

Sadly, many people learn the hard way that every ill-conceived attempt to eliminate dissatisfaction through earthly things leads only to a further and deeper level of this intolerable affliction. Sadder still, there are many who would forfeit their soul just to avoid the bitter taste of dissatisfaction. How troubling this is, especially when "blessed dissatisfaction" can lead us elsewhere. In a passage from his *Diary of a Russian Priest,* Fr Alexander Elchaninov eloquently describes the transition from dissatisfaction to satisfaction.

> What is this continual sense of dissatisfaction, of anxiety, which we normally feel within us, save the stifled voice of conscience speaking to us inwardly on the subconscious level, and often contradicting our own will and declaring the untruth that our life is? As long as we live in conflict with the law of light which has been granted us, this voice will not be silent, for it is the voice of God Himself in our soul. On the other hand, that rare feeling of keen satisfaction, of plenitude and joy, is the happiness caused by the union of the divine principle in our soul with the universal harmony and the divine essence of the world.[*]

If the living God exists, as we believe He does, how could we *not* feel dissatisfied by His absence from our lives? What could possibly fill the enormous space in the depth of our hearts that yearns for God *"as a hart longs for flowing streams"* (Ps 42.1)? It is as if when people hear the voice of God calling them – in their heart, their conscience, through another person, or through a personal tragedy – they turn up the volume to drown out that call. If we were made for God, then each person has an "instinct for the transcendent" (to borrow an expression I remember Fr Alexander Schmemann using) that can only be suppressed at an incalculable cost to our very humanity. In His infinite mercy, the Lord blesses us with a feeling of dissatisfaction so we do not foolishly lose our souls in the infinitesimal pseudo-satisfactions that come our way. Therefore, we thank God for the gift of "blessed dissatisfaction."

When we realize that we "can't get no satisfaction," we have approached the threshold of making a meaningful decision about

---

[*] (Crestwood, NY: St Vladimir's Seminary Press, 2001), 26.

the direction of our life. The way "down" can lead to the kind of benign despair that characterizes the lives of many today. The way "up," on the other hand, leads to the one who "alone has immortality and dwells in unapproachable light" (1 Tim 6.16). The Rolling Stones uncovered the truth of an enduring condition that we all must face and deal with. I am not so sure about the solution they would ultimately offer, but their initial intuition proved to be very "Orthodox."

The Fourth Monday of July
Originally Written: July 2015

A Feast of Divine Beauty

The Feast of the Transfiguration of the Lord, a feast of light and glory, is celebrated every year on August 6. The account of the Transfiguration can be found in three of the Gospels – Matthew 17.1–9, Mark 9.2–8, and Luke 9.28–36. There is also a powerful eyewitness account of the event written by the Apostle Peter in 2 Peter 1.10–19. These scriptural accounts deserve a careful and prayerful reading. The transfigured Lord reveals the splendor of a human being fully alive, for Christ reveals to us the perfect image of humanity transfigured by the glory of God. That is why "His face shone like the sun, and his garments became white as light" (Mt 17.2). The hymnography of the Feast makes this point repeatedly:

> In His own person He showed them the nature of man, arrayed in the original beauty of the image.... Thou hast made the nature that had grown dark in Adam to shine again as lightning transforming it into the glory and splendor of Thy divinity." (Vespers Aposticha of the Feast)

On Mount Tabor, Christ revealed both our origin and our destiny. As the "radiance of the Father" (Heb 1.3), He is the perfect and natural icon, or image, of the invisible God (Col 1.15). As human beings created according to the image and likeness of God, we are essentially "images of the Image." What Christ is, by nature, is what we are meant to be by grace – "partakers of the divine nature" (1 Pet 1.4). This is promised and pledged to us in the age to come, when "the righteous will shine like the sun in the kingdom of their Father" (Mt 13.43), but revealed now in Christ, who is the incarnate Son of God – a revelation, no doubt, of extraordinary beauty. Thus, the Transfiguration is a feast of divine beauty. Can anything more splendid possibly be envisioned?

In other words, whatever Christ does or says is what a perfect human being united to God would do or say. He not only reveals God to us, but also humanity. Look at Christ and you are looking at what it means to be truly and genuinely human. He is what Adam was meant to be, but failed to be because of sin. As Christ is without sin, He is the last (and perfect) Adam. He is also the "man of heaven" because He reveals to us what heaven is like, where we will bear His image (1 Cor 15.47–49). All of this was revealed to the disciples on Mount Tabor when, with even more than the dazzling and startling power of an unexpected flash of lightning, Christ was "transfigured before them." In that glorious splendor, the disciples Peter, James and John received a glimpse of the end of time before it had come. That is a good deal to take in at once, so it is no wonder that the disciples "fell on their faces and were filled with awe" (Mt 17.2, 6). It is simultaneously no wonder that Peter made a suggestion to the Lord – "I will make three booths" – in the hope of prolonging this experience. Through them, and our celebration of the feast, we receive that same glimpse. The King reveals to us His kingdom, so that we may be attracted to it and then live for it. In that sense, as Christians, we are future-oriented.

But if Christ is the perfect human being, then He is such because of His obedience to His heavenly Father. He is always "obedient unto death, even death on a cross" (Phil 2.8). Therefore, the Lord came down from the mountain. Neither He nor the disciples could linger there – He had yet to accomplish His "exodus" at Jerusalem (Lk 9.31). This is clearly an allusion to the cross and resurrection. In fact, Christ was "made perfect" because "He learned obedience through what he suffered" (Heb 5.8–9). Christ was never *not* obedient to His Father! He always said to His heavenly Father, "not my will, but Thine, be done" (Lk 22.42). His authority and glory are firmly grounded in that obedience. The result (and consequence) of this obedience is expressed by the Apostle Paul by his use of the word "therefore" in the following passage:

> Therefore God has highly exalted him and bestowed on him the name which is above every name, that at the name of Jesus every knee should bow, in heaven and on earth and under the earth, and every tongue confess that Jesus Christ is Lord, to the glory of God the Father. (Phil 2.9–11)

St Paul, however, is not finished with drawing out further consequences for us with another "therefore" as he continues,

> Therefore, my beloved, as you have always obeyed, so now, not only as in my presence but much more in my absence, work out your own salvation with fear and trembling, for God is at work in you, both to will and to work for his good pleasure. (Phil 2.12–13)

It seems rather clear, then, that we must be obedient to God – like Christ was at all times and in all things – if we are to share in His glory at the end of time.

The First Monday of August
Originally Written: August 2013

The Dormition Fast: Commitment Versus Convenience

August 1 is the beginning of the relatively short Dormition Fast that concludes with the celebration of the Great Feast of the Dormition on August 15. As we contemplate our own destiny in that of the Theotokos, it is theologically and spiritually appropriate that we understand this to be the culmination of the liturgical year. The preparatory fast is well-placed, falling as it does at the midpoint of summer. Coming after the relatively slow and liturgically "silent" month of July, the ascetical effort we are now called to embrace can lift us out of any spiritual torpor that may be afflicting us. This is especially true if the summer heat has taken its toll on us both physically and spiritually. Spiritual vigilance can replace the apathy and indifference that so often clings to us this time of year. As we honor the translation of the Mother of God into the eternal life of the kingdom of heaven, we simultaneously encounter spiritual renewal through the time-honored and life-affirming practices of prayer, almsgiving, and fasting (Mt 6.1–18).

Yet, every fast confronts us with both a challenge and a choice. In this instance, I would say that our choice is between "convenience" and "commitment." We can choose convenience because of the simple fact that fasting is decidedly *in*convenient. It takes planning, vigilance, discipline, self-denial, and a concerted effort. It is convenient to allow life to flow on at its usual (summer) rhythm, which often includes seeking the path of least resistance. Breaking our established patterns of living is always difficult, and it may be something we would only contemplate with reluctance. Perhaps we need to admit that, as middle-class Americans, we are impatient with inconvenience, since just about every aspect of our lives today is meant to amplify convenience as a "mode of existence" we need to embrace "religiously." We may think and feel that we are entitled to live by the "philosophy" of convenience. One choice, then, is to do nothing different during this current Dormition Fast, or perhaps only something minimal – a kind of token recognition of our life in the Church. I am not quite sure, however, what such a choice would yield in terms of furthering our growth "in Christ." It may amount to little more than a missed opportunity.

Yet the choice remains to embrace the Dormition Fast, a choice that is decidedly counter-cultural and one that manifests a conscious commitment to an Orthodox Christian way of life. To be committed means to care – the spiritual antidote to the passion of *acedia* which literally means "not caring." Such a commitment signifies that we are looking beyond what is convenient toward what is meaningful. It would be a choice in which we recognize our weaknesses, and our need to discern the "mind of Christ," however inconvenient that process may be. And this we have as a gift within the life of the Church. It is a difficult choice to make, and one that is perhaps particularly difficult within the life of a family with children who are often resistant to change. I still believe, though, that such a commitment will bear fruit in our families and in our parishes. (If embraced legalistically and judgmentally, however, we will forfeit our access to the potential fruitfulness of the fast and only succeed in creating a miserable atmosphere in our homes). It is a choice that is determined to seize a good opportunity as at least a potential tool that leads to spiritual growth.

My observation is that we tend to combine convenience and commitment in our contemporary life. We often don't allow the Church to "get in the way" of our plans and goals and admittedly there are times when that may be hard to avoid in certain circumstances. Yet, viewing the Church as our "second choice" may easily harden into an automatic and unchallenged principle –

it is hard to prevail in the never-ending "battle of the calendars." The surrounding social and cultural milieu no longer supports our commitment to Christ and the Church. In fact, it is usually quite indifferent and it may even be hostile toward such a commitment. Though we may hesitate to admit it, it is quite a challenge to withstand conforming to the world around us. But it is never impossible to choose our commitment to our Orthodox Christian way of life over what is merely convenient – or simply desired. This dilemma of sorts may just be one of those "daily crosses" that the Lord spoke of (although it may be a stretch to call that a cross). Bearing this cross also entails choices, and we must assess these choices with honesty as we look at all the factors that make up our lives. In short, it is difficult – but profoundly rewarding – to practice our Orthodox Christian faith today.

I remain confident, however, that the heart of a sincere Orthodox Christian desires to choose the hard path of commitment over the easy (and rather boring?) path of convenience. We now have the God-given opportunity to escape the summer doldrums that drain our spiritual energy. With prayer, almsgiving, and fasting, we can renew our tired bodies and souls. We can lift our "drooping hands" and strengthen our "weak knees" (Heb 12.12) in an attitude of prayer and thanksgiving. The Dormition of the Theotokos has often been called the "summer Pascha." It celebrates the victory of life over death – or of death as a translation into the kingdom of heaven. The Dormition Fast prepares us in spiritual vigilance for that glorious celebration. "Behold, now is the acceptable time; behold now is the day of salvation!" (2 Cor 6.2).

The Second Monday of August
Originally Written: August 2011

The Awesome God and the Transfigured Life

Look down from heaven, O Master, upon those who have bowed their heads unto Thee, the awesome God.
(From the Divine Liturgy)

The Afterfeast of the Transfiguration of Christ continues until its leavetaking on August 13. Having ascended Mount Tabor with the disciples of the Lord, we will then descend back into the world to hopefully bear witness to the glorious vision that has been vouchsafed to us of Christ shining resplendently in His divine glory (Mk 9.1–8; Mt 17.1–13; Lk 9.28–36). Biblically, the "glory of God," refers to a palpable "shining forth" of the presence of God that overwhelms the recipient of such a vision. Their spiritual senses purified by the grace of the Holy Spirit, the disciples could "see" the glory of God revealed in Christ on Mount Tabor, and they, too, were overwhelmed. Truly, therefore, the transfiguration is an "awesome" feast.

Yet, today, everything is described as "awesome": the loud, the superficial, the mundane. Are we witnessing a kind of experiential egalitarianism, where nothing stands apart from or above anything else? Is even the awesomeness of God succumbing to this leveling effect? How discouraging that would be, for we refer to God liturgically as "the awesome Judge," the "awesome God;" and the Eucharist as the "awesome mysteries of Christ." This is as it should be, for the word awesome – based on the noun "awe" – continues to be defined today as "an emotion variously combining dread, veneration, and wonder that is inspired by authority or by the sacred or sublime." It is God who is truly awesome – anything else that can be genuinely described as awesome derives that quality from God.

More specifically, has the awesomeness of the Transfiguration been reduced to yet another passing "church event" that comes and goes with an alarmingly insignificant amount of impact on our minds and hearts? Can the awesome Feast of the Transfiguration even "compete" any longer with the latest movie for our attentions, or our capacity as human beings to be "awed" by the sacred and sublime? I am convinced that when everything is "awesome," nothing is really awesome. Inevitably, we will find ourselves calling the most boring of occurrences "awesome," but with no real enthusiasm or conviction. (Perhaps we can excuse our younger children who are now using the term "awesome," for the little things in life can still fill them with a sense of wonder that we adults have lost.)

Be that as it may, the disciples were awed by Christ on Mount Tabor when "He was transfigured before them, and his face shone like the sun, and his garments became white as light" (Mt 17.2). This metamorphosis – the Greek word behind our transfiguration – was a direct revelation of Christ's divine nature or, more precisely, of the uncreated energies of His divinity which now shone through the flesh He assumed in the incarnation. Jesus did not become something He previously was not, but revealed His true identity as both God and man. To the glory of God, Jesus Christ is a human being fully alive. Such a revelation is unique to the Gospels and clearly prefigures the Lord's resurrection and the glory of the age to come. Moses and Elijah appeared flanking the Lord, "talking with him" (v. 3). Peter wanted to build three booths: one for Christ, one for Moses, and one for Elijah. His intent was to prolong the vision and the experience encountered on Mount Tabor, but this was not to be. Interestingly, in an apocryphal account of the Transfiguration, Peter is openly rebuked for his mistaken desire. Peter and other disciples – James and John – must come down from the mount and witness to Christ through the remainder of their lives and, ultimately, through their death.

The same is true of us. If we have not lost our capacity to be awed in the presence of God (not only in the Liturgy, but also when reading the Scriptures, praying alone, looking into the face of another and seeing the "image and likeness of God" in them), then we must take that awesome experience with us into the everyday flow of events and encounters that mark our lives. We must come down from those metaphorical mountains we climb and bear witness to the experience of the transfigured Lord by the quality of our Christian lives:

> O Christ our God, who was transfigured in glory on Mount Tabor showing to Thy disciples the splendor of Thy Godhead, do Thou enlighten us also with the light of Thy knowledge and guide us in the path of Thy commandments, for Thou alone art good and lovest mankind. (Litiya verse of the Feast of the Transfiguration)

That the transfiguration is considered one of the great and holy feasts of the Church is meaningless if it does not have an impact on us. The goodness, truth, and beauty that shine forth from Christ are the uncreated energies that free us from apathy and cynicism; and free us further to pursue the virtue of Christ that "has covered the heavens" (Liturgy of Preparation in the Divine Liturgy).

The Third Monday of August
Originally Written: August 2009

Rejoicing in the "Deathless Death"

Words cannot attain to what is beyond speech, just as eyes cannot stare at the sun. But though it is impossible for us to tell of things surpassing words, we can, by the love of those we extol, sing their praises, and we may use words to pay our debt, and express our longing for the Mother of God in hymns as best we can, without in any way touching the intangible.

– St Gregory Palamas, *Homily On the Dormition*

As I occasionally like to point out, the twelve major feast days of the Church year do not simply "come and go" in a twenty-four-hour period – if you glance at a church calendar, you may come across the following notations when encountering a major feast: "forefeast," "afterfeast," and "leavetaking" (of the feast). In fact, the feast we are now continuing to celebrate – the Dormition of the Theotokos (August 15) – is preceded by one day of forefeast (August 14) and followed by eight days of afterfeast (August 16-23).

This is the "longest" feast dedicated to the Mother of God in terms of duration and the "leavetaking" occurs on August 23. Therefore, we will again have the joy of expressing "our longing for the Mother of God in hymns as best we can," as St Gregory Palamas so eloquently stated. This has been the case throughout this past week, as the Church allows us to further contemplate and experience the mystery of the falling asleep of the Theotokos and its bearing on our lives. There is nothing more "theo-logical" than connecting the life and death of the Mother of God with that of her Son and Savior, our Lord Jesus Christ. The Lord did not "pass through" His mother, but was truly born of her, "ineffably" and "without seed" as we sing and chant when praising this great mystery of the Incarnation. The Mother of God held her Son in her arms when He was born, and when she is "born" into the new life of the kingdom of God, her Son bears her soul in his arms:

> She who is higher than the heavens and more glorious than the cherubim, she who is held in greater honor than all creation, she who by reason of her surpassing purity became the receiver of the everlasting Essence, today commends her most pure soul into the hands of her Son. With her all things are filled with joy and she bestows great mercy upon us.
>
> Sing, O ye people, sing ye the praises of the Mother of our God: for today she delivers her soul, full of light, into the immaculate hands of Him who was made incarnate of her without seed. (Litiya at Great Vespers)

But since the Mother of God is not the "great exception" but rather the "great example," as Fr Schmemann was fond of saying, she embodies our greatest longing and hope for human beings created in the image and likeness of God. Her life exemplifies the beauty of "falling asleep" in the Lord surrounded by our loved ones, as she was surrounded by the apostles and friends, according to tradition. She teaches us to offer our lives to the risen and ever-present Lord as a final eucharistic gift, in the humble assurance that He will receive it and "carry" it into His everlasting Kingdom. In her death, we are reminded that we are buried to the accompaniment of "psalms, hymns, and spiritual songs" (Eph 5.19) that express our belief that death has been overcome in the death and resurrection of Christ. Although not an official dogma of the Church, the belief exists that the Mother of God was bodily "translated" to heaven, since the Lord did not allow the most-pure temple of the Word to experience corruption:

> The Lord and God of all gave thee as thy portion the things that are above nature. For just as He kept thee virgin in thy childbirth so did He preserve thy body incorrupt in the tomb; and He glorified thee by a divine Translation, showing thee honour as a Son to His Mother.
>
> (Matins, First Canon, Canticle Six)

As Archbishop Kallistos says in his explanation of the theological meaning of this feast:

> Orthodox Tradition is clear and unwavering in regard to the central point: the Holy Virgin underwent, as did her Son, a physical death, but her body – like His – was afterwards raised from the dead and she was taken up into heaven, in her body as well as in her soul. She has passed beyond death and judgment, and lives wholly in the Age to Come. The Resurrection of the Body, which all Christians await, has in her case been anticipated and is already an accomplished fact. That does not mean, however, that she is dissociated from the rest of humanity and placed in a wholly different category: for we all hope to share one day in that same glory of the Resurrection of the Body which she enjoys even now.*

However, this affirmation belongs to the inner tradition of the Church and, as stated above, has never been accorded dogmatic status. The Theotokos died according to the necessity that plagues our fallen human nature inherited from of old. Her death, therefore, cannot be termed "voluntary" as the death of her Son was. Her Son, the Lord Jesus Christ, is her Savior, as He is ours. Summing up her exemplary role for all Christians, Fr Thomas Hopko wrote:

> The feast of the Dormition is the sign, the guarantee, and the celebration that Mary's fate is the destiny of all those of "low estate" whose souls magnify the Lord, whose

---

* Mother Mary and Archimandrite Kallistos Ware, *The Festal Menaion*, 64.

spirits rejoice in God the Saviour, whose lives are totally dedicated to hearing and keeping the Word of God which is given to men in Mary's child, the Saviour and Redeemer of the world.*

The feasts of the Church are junctures of theological reflection and existential participation, as they actualize the events of our salvation and deification in the "today" of the Church's ongoing life in the world. We can further rejoice in the "deathless death" of the Theotokos as we come to worship the living God who makes all things possible.

---

* Thomas Hopko, *Worship*, vol. 2 of *The Orthodox Faith* (Crestwood: St Vladimir's Seminary Press, 1984), 145.

The Fourth Monday of August
Originally Written: July 2013

Rejoicing in All that Is Good

In St Paul's Epistle to the Philippians, we find this marvelous passage:

> Finally, brethren, whatever is true, whatever is honorable, whatever is just, whatever is pure, whatever is lovely, whatever is gracious, if there is any excellence, if there is anything worthy of praise, think about these things. (4.8–9)

The apostle exhorts us to "think about these things" – to meditate upon them – a task that may take some effort on our part. For without having time to pause and "think about these things," we may easily lose the inclination to do so. It would be spiritually hazardous to assume that the virtues enumerated in this passage somehow come to us automatically, simply because we are church-going Christians. Hence, it is imperative that we listen to the Apostle Paul and actively "think about these things" – to meditate upon them – and, in so doing, to give ourselves the opportunity to search out all that is wholesome in life.

St Paul essentially borrows this list of virtues commonly found in the various Greek philosophical schools of his cultural milieu. The pursuit of such virtues, it was thought, led to the "good life," for only a life dedicated to these virtues would be worth living. He apparently continued to respect this centuries-old tradition. We should bear this in mind whenever confronted with other religious beliefs or serious philosophical schools of thought – as much as we may disagree with them from our Christian perspective, there is also much to be found in the teachings of other religions and philosophies that is honorable, just, pure, lovely, gracious, excellent, and worthy of praise. To think otherwise would be to succumb to the temptations of a sectarian mind. A sect is a group that cannot find anything of value outside of its own narrowly defined borders. This breeds some form of obscurantism and narrow-mindedness, if not eventually fanaticism. A "catholic" mind, as understood by the great Church fathers, can rejoice in whatever is true, good or beautiful, even if it is found outside the Church. Anecdotally, I recall at time when I was a seminarian, and the theme of the ensuing conversation around us, with Fr John Meyendorff present, prompted him to say: "I like to believe that Mozart will be in the kingdom of heaven because of the beauty of the music that he created." Similarly, I would like to believe that something like this is what the Apostle was alluding to in his celebrated passage from Philippians.

At the same time, St Paul included this exhortation in an epistle that is thoroughly and consistently christocentric. The living reality of Christ permeates all of St Paul's thoughts and actions. There is nothing that is worthy of pursuit that is outside of Christ. For the Apostle Paul, nothing can compare with the knowledge of Christ. And this "knowledge" is not intellectual, but deeply experiential. In one of his most famous passages, he writes:

> But whatever gain I had, I counted as loss for the sake of Christ. Indeed, I count everything as loss because of the surpassing worth of knowing Christ Jesus my Lord. For his sake I have suffered the loss of all things, and count them as refuse [in Greek, *skivala*, i.e., rubbish, dung, excrement] in order that I may gain Christ and be found in him. (Phil 3.7–8)

Anything that is of the truth somehow belongs to Christ and comes from Christ – even if not acknowledged. So, the virtues that St Paul exhorts the Philippians to pursue are found in Christ in a preeminent form. In other words, the classical virtues – though taught and found elsewhere – find their perfect manifestation in

Christ. Yet the point remains that we can rejoice in all that is good, wherever we encounter it. The apostle assures us that with such an approach to life, the "God of peace" indeed will be with us.

With the end of August, we have arrived at the end of the Church year and prepare for the next. We have had every opportunity to deepen our relationship with Christ through the ongoing rhythm of fasting and feasting according to the Church's liturgical calendar and, of course, in the Eucharist, "the sacrament of sacraments." The feasts of the Church and the Liturgy have actualized the presence of Christ and the Theotokos in the midst of the grace-filled life of the Church – "the sanctification of time" as it has been called – and within the depths of our minds and hearts. We have been further nurtured by the word of God as proclaimed in the Holy Scriptures in our liturgical assemblies and in the quiet of our rooms with the door shut. As we live our lives in the surrounding world, perhaps we have been deeply and positively impacted through our human relationships, the beauty of the natural world, or an enduring work of art. We believe that is present in all of "these things."

These God-given encounters reveal to us all that is true, honorable, just, pure, lovely, gracious, excellent, and worthy of praise. In other words, we have had every opportunity to simply become more *human* – and, in becoming more human, we simultaneously draw closer to God. Further, the richness of life presupposes our ever-vigilant struggle against sin and our ongoing repentance. The *Prayer of the Hours* reveals to us the fruits of repentance: to "sanctify our souls, purify our bodies, correct our minds, cleanse our thoughts; and deliver us from all tribulation, evil, and distress." That is indeed a great endeavor, "but with God all things are possible" (Mt 19.27).

Appendix: Reading the Meditations through the Liturgical Year

Nr.	Meditation Title	Placement in Text/Year	Feast / Season
1	The Church New Year: Curing the Summertime Blues	First Monday of September	Indiction (September 1)
2	The Nativity of the Theotokos and Its Synaxis: Remebering Sts Joachim and Anna	Second Monday of September	Nativity of the Theotokos (September 8) Synaxis of Sts Joachim and Anna (September 9)
3	"Wood Is Healed by Wood!"	Third Monday of September	Feast of the Elevation of the Holy Cross (September 14)
4	Before Thy Cross, We Bow Down in Worship!	Fourth Monday in September	Leavetaking of the Feast of the Elevation of the Holy Cross (September 21)
5	Glory to God for Autumn	Fourth Monday of September	Autumn
6	"Let Us Attend!"	First Monday of October	N/A
7	Tribulation in This Life	Second Monday of October	N/A
8	"God or Nothing"	Third Monday of October	N/A
9	Moving beyond Mere Belief	Fourth Monday of October	N/A
10	Eucharistic Beings in a Eucharistic Society	First Monday of November	Twelfth Sunday of Luke/ Sunday of the Ten Lepers

11	Forty Shopping (and Fasting) Days until Christmas	Second Monday of November	Anticipates the start of the Nativity Fast (November 15)
12	Indulging Not in Food, But in Giving Thanks to the Lord	Third Monday of November	U.S. Thanksgiving (third Thursday of November)
13	Preparing for the Incarnation	Fourth Monday of November	Anticipates Christmas
14	The Image of Giving in St Nicholas	First Monday of December	Feast of St Nicholas (December 6)
15	In the Fullness of Time	Second Monday of December	Christmas or the week prior
16	Christmas and Martyrdom	Third Monday of December	Christmas (December 25)
17	The Incarnation: A Word about the Word	Fourth Monday of December	Christmas (December 25)
18	The Time of Our Lives	Fifth Monday of December	Civil New Year (January 1)
19	Redeeming the Time	First Monday of January	Civil New Year (January 1)
20	Baptism: "When All Is Said and Done"	Second Monday of January	N/A
21	Rebuking the Tempter and Following Jesus	Third Monday of January	Leavetaking of Theophany (January 14)
22	A "Pouring Out of Long Accumulating, Long Pent-up Pain"	Fourth Monday of January	N/A
23	Ascending with Zacchaeus	Fifth Monday of January	The Sunday of Zacchaeus, the first pre-lenten Sunday
24	If St John Chrysostom Had Watched the Super Bowl	First Monday of February	U.S. Super Bowl (first Sunday of February)

25	An Infant's Burial	Second Monday of February	N/A
26	The Heresy of the Rapture	Third Monday of February	N/A
27	Now Is the Acceptable Time: Lent as Beginning	Fourth Monday of February	Clean Monday
28	On the Liturgy of St Basil the Great	First Monday of March	Great Lent
29	To Refresh Our Souls and Encourage Us	Second Monday of March	Sunday of the Life-Giving Cross (Third Week of Lent)
30	The Announcement of the Incarnation	Third Monday of March	The Feast of the Annunciation (March 25)
31	The Real Stairway to Heaven	Fourth Monday of March	Great Lent
32	*Acedia*, Us, and Our Lenten Effort	First Monday of April	Great Lent
33	Holy Week: A Mystic Torrent	Second Monday of April	Holy Week
34	The Resurrection of Christ and the Rise of Christianity	Third Monday of April	Pascha
35	Paschal Reminiscences	Fourth Monday of April	Pascha
36	"Lent after Lent" and "Life after Pascha"	First Monday of May	Paschal Season
37	Death's Dominion Has Been Shattered!	Second Monday of May	Paschal Season
38	"Do You Want to Be Healed?"	Third Monday of May	Paschal Season
39	Mid-Pentecost: "Glistening with Splendor"	Fourth Monday of May	Mid-Pentecost
40	From Where Do We Draw Our Water?	Fifth Monday of May	Sunday of the Samaritan Woman (Fifth Sunday after Pascha)
41	Too Busy NOT to Pray	First Monday of June	N/A

42	Forty-Nine Plus One: Pentecost and the Life beyond Time	Second Monday of June	Pentecost (50 Days after Pascha)
43	The Day of the Holy Spirit	Third Monday of June	Pentecost Monday (Day of the Holy Spirit)
44	Finding our "Self" in the Other: Reflections on National Selfie Day	Fourth Monday of June	National Selfie Day (June 21)
45	July: A Month-Long Spiritual Desert	First Monday of July	July
46	Bored by Sin	Second Monday of July	Summer
47	Blessed Dissatisfaction	Third Monday of July	Summer
48	A Feast of Divine Beauty	Fourth Monday of July	Anticipates the Feast of the Transfiguration (August 6)
49	The Dormition Fast: Commitment Versus Convenience	First Monday of August	Dormition Fast (August 1-15)
50	The Awesome God and the Transfigured Life	Second Monday of August	Leavetaking of the Transfiguration (August 13)
51	Rejoicing in the Deathless Death	Third Monday of August	Feast of the Dormition (August 15)
52	Rejoicing in All that Is Good	Fourth Monday of August	N/A

CPSIA information can be obtained
at www.ICGtesting.com
Printed in the USA
FFHW02n1216300918
48637162-52601FF